Leckie✕Leckie

Scotland's leading educational publishers

CfE Higher
BUSINESS MANAGEMENT
SUCCESS GUIDE

CfE Higher BUSINESS MANAGEMENT SUCCESS GUIDE

Derek McInally and Anne Ross

Contents

Preparing for Higher Business Management

Business Management Assignment

Understanding Business

Management of People and Finance

Management of Marketing and Operations

About this Success Guide

This *Success Guide* is structured around the three Units of the Higher Business Management course, and breaks down the course content into small manageable sections for you to revise. There are examples of **Sample examination questions** together with **Quick fire questions** for you to complete with answers from page 114 onwards. Throughout the *Success Guide*, you will find **Top Tips** for you to read and take note of.

TOP TIP

The Quick Fire Questions can be done on your own – or better still, get a friend to test you on the different sections.

This *Success Guide* revision book is designed to give you the essential knowledge to help you prepare for the Unit Assessments, the Assignment and your SQA question paper.

While this *Success Guide* can be used on its own, it would prove helpful to use it along with the *Business Management Course Notes*. The *Course Notes* encourage you to keep a learning log during your study of Higher Business Management. This *Success Guide* can help you with the log, as it summaries the topics in each of the Units.

Higher Business Management

The study of Business Management has become increasingly popular and is recognised as a valuable qualification for most courses in Further and Higher Education. Many students starting to study Higher Business Management will already have completed the National 5 level course (N5). Higher Business Management builds on the skills, knowledge and understanding gained at N5, but it is recognised that for many students this will be a 'crash' subject and Business Management has proved an immensely popular and successful course choice for those needing to get a good grade in a Higher subject.

The content of Higher Business Management demonstrates how large organisations operate and the steps they take to achieve their objectives. The Higher Business Management course is designed to combine theoretical and practical aspects of learning through the use of real-life business contexts.

Studying Higher Business Management will help you understand and make use of business information to interpret and report on a range of large organisations in the private, public and third sectors.

No one comes to Business Management without some knowledge and appreciation of business in society and how it directly impacts upon them as a consumer. The purpose of the course is to deepen that understanding and provide a more mature understanding by introducing the student to common business approaches and theoretical models of best business practice.

The coverage of skills for learning, skills for life and skills for work are illustrated in the table below.

Skill	How it is developed
Literacy	• writing answers to questions in Unit and Course assessments • watching and listening to news reports on business • reading newspaper articles • communicating through presentations/working in groups/discussions/question and answer sessions • evaluating self and peers • presenting findings from research in a coherent format
Numeracy	• carrying out calculations, for example when completing a cash budget, financial records and calculating ratios • gathering and interpreting numerical information from a range of sources and presenting it in a table, graph or diagram to aid interpretation
Employability, enterprise and citizenship	• demonstrating an understanding of how businesses work, particularly when looking at working practices, business structures and customer satisfaction • encouraging autonomy/initiative through personal research • developing skills to allow the student to enter the world of work, such as exploring career opportunities • improving ICT skills for a technology-driven society • working with others • using initiative and innovation, and displaying creativity, flexibility and resourcefulness, for example when working in groups • meeting deadlines, being proactive in roles and being part of a team
Thinking skills	• using business vocabulary • using case studies/scenarios • setting concepts in real-life examples • completing personal research and team-working • sharing information and explaining its importance • using information to solve problems • planning, organising and completing tasks

Adapted from SQA Course Support Notes for Higher Business Management

The course builds upon the National 5 Business Management course, which has a focus on small to medium size business structures. The Higher focuses on large organisations. The Higher course assumes you will also have a solid understanding of course content at National 5 level.

TOP TIP

Why not buy the Success Guide for National 5 Business Management for some background reading?

Course structure

Unit 1	Understanding Business	• Unit 1 explores the ways in which large organisations in the private, public and third sectors operate. It examines the objectives of these organisations and the way in which they are structured. • It analyses and evaluates the impact that the external environment has on an organisation's activity, and considers the implications that a range of internal constraints have on decision-making. • It also explores the interest and impact of stakeholders.
Unit 2	Management of People and Finance	• Unit 2 can be more easily understood by breaking it down into two areas: the management of people and management of finance. • In the management of people, sometimes referred to as Human Resources, it emphasises the ways in which employees contribute to the success of large organisations, including leadership, motivation, employee relations and current employment legislation. • In the management of finance, it identifies sources of finance for large organisations and also covers how final statements (trading, profit and loss and balance sheets) are used to support decision-making. • In this and in the next unit, the impacts of existing and emerging technologies are explored.
Unit 3	Management of Marketing and Operations	• Unit 3 can also be broken down into two areas: marketing and operations. • Through marketing Unit 3 emphasises the importance of satisfying both internal and external customers' needs. • It covers how these needs are met through the production process under operations. • It also covers existing and emerging technologies and how they can improve business practice.

Course and Unit assessment

Course Assessment structure

Assignment	30 marks
Question paper	70 marks
	Total 100 marks

Assignment

This is completed in class and is worth 30% of your overall grade. It is submitted to the SQA for marking. The Assignment consists of:

- studying a large business
- recommending a course of action to improve business activity
- interpreting and evaluating both primary and/or secondary data
- producing a report on your recommendations or observations

The Assignment component will have 30 marks (30% of the total mark). There is a chapter in this Success Guide dedicated to the Assignment.

Question paper

This is sat under examination conditions during the SQA exam and will last for **2 hours 15 minutes**.

TOP TIP

Start early to gather information on a number of large businesses. This will help you make the final decision of which business and which aspect of the organisation you wish to report on. Keep the details of the businesses in your learning log.

Section 1	The case study is worth 30 marks and consists of a set of short-answer questions based on a business case study stimulus.
	The questions will be drawn from any aspect of the Course, with most questions to be answered in the context of the type of business in the case study.
Section 2	This section is worth 40 marks and consists of four extended response questions of 10 marks each that will be split into sub-questions as appropriate. The questions will be thematic or context-based, for example on marketing, finance, business objectives, the role of technology in business. The questions will assess knowledge and understanding, and application of knowledge and understanding.

You will be graded in the course assessment from A to D.

Unit Assessment

TOP TIP

The Unit Assessment ensures that you have minimum competency of the course content. Would you fly in a plane where the pilot was described as having 'minimum competency'? Aim higher than Unit passes.

To gain the award for the Course you must pass the requirements of the Unit Assessments. Success is measured as a pass or a fail.

These are made up of outcomes, which are broken down into Assessment Standards for each of the three Units. A pass is regarded as minimum competency of the course content and is achieved by matching evidence against the Assessment Standards. You can do this by compiling a portfolio of naturally occurring evidence during the year, or undertaking tasks that assess proficiency across two or more of the Units, or more simply by completing exercises on a Unit-by-Unit approach. Your teacher/lecturer will direct you.

Command words

Extract from an SQA External Assessment Report:

> *Candidates who know how to handle the list of command words perform significantly better than those who do not.*

The questions you encounter in Higher Business Management use 'command' words. A command is not a polite request – it is a **demand**. Therefore when you come across 'command' words in assessments, you ignore them at your peril.

Frequently, a question might contain more than one command word, so be careful that you are answering the full question and not simply one part of it.

TOP TIP

Underline or highlight the command word(s) used in questions to ensure that you focus on how you are expected to answer. Take care to make sure that your response to a question is really what is **actually** asked.

Below is a list of the command words used during assessment. Learn their meaning. Use this list whenever you are answering a question until you are familiar with the meaning of each command.

Command word	Definition
Compare	Point out similarities and differences between two or more factors. You might also be asked to state a preference. You should try to emphasise or state the unique features of each in comparison to the other(s).
Example	**Compare stakeholders' conflict and how stakeholders might resolve such conflict.**
Describe	Provide a detailed factual description. One-word answers for 'descriptions' are never acceptable, you must use a sentence(s). You can describe characteristics and/or features appropriate to the question asked. While examples are not usually credited in Higher Business Management, you may find they help you in a description. You may provide a number of straightforward points or a smaller number of developed points, or a combination of these. Be guided by the number of marks being awarded.
Example	**Describe the people, process and physical evidence used by a multinational company you are familiar with.**
Discuss	Examine closely, taking account of strengths and weaknesses in an argument (for and against). This cannot simply be a list – points must be developed. Although negatives and positives should be explored, it is not necessary in all cases. It is important that you carefully read and fully understand the question being asked.
Example	**Discuss the place technology can play in deciding on a pricing strategy.**

Command word	Definition
Explain	Give a detailed explanation of the impact of some course of action. You must make the relationship clear between action and impact. Give reasons for your points – again remember that sometimes giving examples can help the examiner understand what you are writing about. You may provide a number of straightforward points of explanation or a smaller number of developed points, or a combination of these – again be guided by the mark allocation.
Example	**Explain the importance of ethical practices in developing positive customer relations.**
Advantage and disadvantage (can be used with describe, discuss, explain)	Pros and cons of something – at least one advantage and one disadvantage should be given to get the full mark allocation. However you need to take care that you do not just give a straight negative of an advantage as a disadvantage – this will not gain any marks. Points must be described, discussed or explained.
Example	**Describe the advantages and disadvantages of branding to an organisation.**

During Unit Assessments you might be asked to **'identify'**. This simply means to name or state and does not require any detail to your answer.

TOP TIP

Avoid using bulleted lists with one or two words – it is too easy to miss out on enough detail to be awarded the full marks. Remember that the marks awarded to questions are an indication of the depth of answer being looked for by the examiner.

TOP TIP

Marks will be awarded for the further development of a point, but make sure that you are actually saying something different and not simply rephrasing an existing statement.

Assignment

It is never too early to start the process of planning your Higher Business Management Assignment.

The Assignment will take the form of a report on an enterprise. An issue will be identified and, following market research, conclusions drawn and recommendations made. This Assignment counts for 30% of the overall SQA mark and therefore it is vital to secure high marks if you hope to achieve a good grade in Higher Business Management.

Assignments are submitted to the SQA for marking towards the end of the course, but the SQA have made the marking scheme quite clear, and so by following some general principles a high mark can be assured.

> **TOP TIP**
>
> Make sure you use the section headings in your report as marks are allocated for the appropriate use of headings.

Step 1

Choose a business and identify an issue or a problem with the enterprise that you wish to base your investigation and conclusions or recommendations on.

This is the crucial stage and your whole Assignment will rest on choosing an appropriate business venture.

Higher Business Management focuses on large businesses, so choose an enterprise that has a medium-to-large operation. There is no need to be concerned with structure of ownership, although a sole trader might not be able to provide enough sources of information for you to build a report on. It can be any of the following:

- private limited company
- public limited company
- charity
- social enterprise
- local or national government organisation.

> **TOP TIP**
>
> Ensure that your chosen business communicates via social media such as Facebook, Twitter and has a website. These will provide good sources of data.

Step 2

Decide on some aspect of the enterprise to report on. At this point you should do some background research to see if there is data out there that links your business with the topic. If not **change** the business, the topic or both!

Suitable topics could be:

- quality measures to be adopted to ensure customer satisfaction
- pricing strategies
- benefits of social responsibility
- sources of finance to support expansion
- developing product/service ranges
- mergers or takeovers.

> **TOP TIP**
>
> Try and ensure that when you type the topic into a search engine your business name or industry receives hits.

Step 3

Choose a business analytical tool that will be most suitable for your chosen issue. An analytical tool is simply a formal process used by businesses to firstly gather data, draw conclusions and then make recommendations from.

It would be advisable to start – as early as possible – to gather articles, news reports, press releases, government statistics etc. on your business and on the topic you are going to investigate. Some of these will be refined into the analytical model of your choice while other sources of data can be used for the next stage of research. The final version of your analytical tool should be included as an Appendix.

Your lecturer/teacher will give you advice on the different types of analytical techniques that can be adopted and what would be most suited for your investigation.

Examples of analytical tools are:

- PESTEC
- SWOT
- production processes
- ratio analysis
- workforce planning
- quality measures
- product life cycle extensions
- Force Field analysis.

You will be expected to explain what your chosen tool shows and how it will be used to support your conclusions and recommendation.

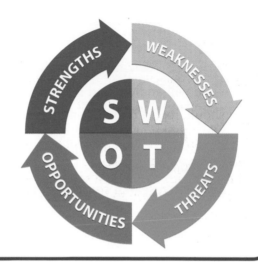

Step 4

Decide on the sources of information you will need to use and how you will collect the information. You should use a minimum of two research sources.

You will be expected to identify the sources used, but the important aspect is why you used them.

Explain why you chose the source:

- why the information found would be of use in terms of your report
- the credibility of the source.

Do not simply repeat a list of common phrases like *reliable, relevant, up-to-date, objective, accurate, biased*, but link it directly to your investigation and say why in this case it was (for example) *relevant*. Here is an example.

The first research source I used was the business website www.tesco.com.

I chose this website as it was entirely relevant to my report because it is the business' own website. I used the website to gather details of the wide range of products that Tesco has for sale, to help me identify the extent of their product portfolio. The information was accurate as it is constantly being updated and it gave me prices as well. However, some information about the business could be biased, such as the 'price promise' in order to attract potential customers.

The second research source I used was the BBC news site www.bbc.co.uk/news.

I chose this website because it contained information about the economy and effects of the recession on business. I gathered statistics and graphs to show the number of businesses that went bankrupt during the last five years. This is relevant to my investigation on 'recession'. The BBC news site is reliable, unbiased and up-to-date. I had confidence that the information was from a reliable source as journalists for the BBC are employed to be impartial.

Reference to the research evidence, for example questionnaires or websites, should be put into an Appendix.

Step 5

Here you will analyse and interpret the research sources and information gathered.

You should report on your findings in relation to the issue you are investigating, and the analytical tool you are using. Your findings should be in-depth and comprehensive. It would add weight to your findings if different sources supported the same conclusion. Here are some examples:

From my research source 1 (the business website) *I found out that:*

Pricing strategies used vary from one season of the year to another according to customer demand for certain products. For example, in summer there is more demand for cold drinks and ice-cream, therefore these products were not selected for promotional pricing strategies.

From my research source 2 (survey) *I found out that:*
- *60% of customers had complained in the last three months*
- *45% of customers had complained in the last two months*
- *30% of customers had complained in the last month.*

This is shown in the graph/pie chart. This means that the business is not meeting their needs and must address the issues they are complaining about quickly, in order to restore customer confidence in the business.

From my research source 3 (newspaper article) *I found out that the PESTEC factors on the decline in holidays taken in the UK were:*
- *Political: the government had not increased the minimum wage rate very much in the last two years*
- *Economic: unemployment figures showed that ...*
- *Social: more and more people enjoy holidays abroad*
- *Technological: mobile devices, laptops etc. make it easier to stay in touch on holiday abroad*

- *Environmental: the last two summers have been the wettest on record in the UK, encouraging people to book foreign holidays*
- *Competition: there is so much choice in terms of tour companies that prices are very competitive.*

Here are some other sample phrases you can use to demonstrate that you have analysed and interpreted your findings:

I noticed that the business … this therefore means that …

It was clear from the pictures/graph/table on the website that …

From the feedback page on the website I found out that customers said … this means that …

My survey results show that x% of respondents are unhappy … this means that the business will have to …

The article in the newspaper proves that …

Overall my evidence shows that …

I am confident that these figures mean that …

Step 6

Identify conclusions and recommendation based on your evidence and the analysis you have undertaken. These should relate to the overall purpose of the report but also how they might meet the needs of internal or external stakeholders. Sample phrases:

I have come to the conclusion that xxxx business should …

I suggest that the business does …

Summing up my evidence, the conclusions I can make are …

I would recommend that the business does the following …

The business should think about doing …

The course of action the business should now take is to …

The business should offer…

ANSWERS | FINDINGS
CONCLUSIONS | RESULTS
SOLUTIONS | OUTCOMES

However, each conclusion or recommendation should be based on your evidence and have a justification or explanation of the effect it will have, for example:

Based on the findings from the business website I suggest that the business conducts training for its employees on customer service. This should mean that the number of complaints reduce, and that customers will be happy to return and shop there again.

The course of action that the business should now take is to expand their product range to appeal to an older segment of the market, for example the 65–75 age group. This will address the lack of sales to customers in this segment of the market.

I recommend that the business employs more staff in the Operations department to carry out quality assurance. Quality assurance checks will mean that fewer problems are identified at the end of the production process and there will be no need for product recalls in the future.

Step 7

The assignment report should be arranged under the following headings:

- Introduction
- Research
- Analysis and interpretation
- Conclusions and recommendations
- Appendix.

It should be word processed formatted in 1.5 line spacing and, depending on font and line spacing, should be about 6–10 pages long (*marks will be deducted if the report is not concise*).

Include graphs, charts, tables, statistics and images that will enhance the quality and presentation of the report.

There should be no more than four appendices. They can include notes, pictures, tables, graphs, charts, questionnaires, as well as lists of website, books, and articles. Make sure that you reference the appendices so that it is clear what research you are referring to.

A set of SQA assessment instructions (known as Appendix 1) will be given to you by your teacher/lecturer prior to completion of the Assignment report.

Use the checklist on the following page to mark your Assignment report against the criteria used by the SQA. Ensure that you are meeting the minimum standards and then try to exceed the criteria by providing more than the minimum.

> **TOP TIP**
>
> Use appropriate business terminology throughout the Report as marks are awarded for appropriate business terms.

Title page

This should include the name of the enterprise. You should include a general picture or company logo. Your name and school/centre should be clearly displayed.

Introduction (3 marks)

Start by stating the aim of the investigation. Also include some justification related to the enterprise. This will gain you 1 mark.

Provide details of the analytical technique used in Step 3. Reference should be made to Appendix 2, where full detailed notes should be held.

Justify the use of this analytical technique in investigating the issue.

Research (4 marks)

Provide a minimum of two sources of information. Market research can be primary, secondary or a combination of both.

Marks are awarded for relevance of the information and the value of this information. Remember: make the value relevant to your situation.

Reference to sources of research should be made to Appendix 3.

Analysis and interpretation (12 marks)

Marks will be credited for each interpretation you make but it must be linked to the market research or the analytical technique used.

You will be awarded marks even if you state your research was inconclusive, as long as it is justified.

Conclusions and recommendations (8 marks)

One mark will be given per conclusion and/or recommendation that is directly linked to the research undertaken. **You must make the link explicit**.

Appendix 1

Synopsis/setting the scene:

*   provide a brief summary of the history of the business and location(s)
*   give a short description of the activities the enterprise is engaged in, along with a statement of the business structure, for example, public limited company, social enterprise, etc.

Appendix 2

Include details of the analytical tool used. You might, for example, show a SWOT analysis.

Appendix 3

Include details of research gathered. For example, questionnaire and/or URL of websites used.

Appendix 4

You can include one more Appendix of your choice.

Collating and reporting (3 marks)

*   One mark will be awarded for the use of headings.
*   One mark for business terminology being correctly applied.
*   One mark for the report being an appropriate length (not too long or too short).

> **TOP TIP**
>
> While an Appendix will not receive any marks in your report, it is normally the first place the SQA Marker will look to get an outline of the business.

The role of business in society

Entrepreneurs are people who think of an idea and go on to develop the idea into a business. Entrepreneurs provide and/or source other essential resources (**inputs**), before focusing these different ingredients into a business enterprise (**process**), in order to provide a good or a service (**output**).

TOP TIP

The role of an entrepreneur is very different from that of a manager. Entrepreneurs create the business while managers sustain the business.

Wealth creation

Entrepreneurs combine together the four **factors of production** to produce goods or services. While all four factors must be present, the importance – or contribution – of each factor will depend upon what is being provided.

Factors of production	Description
Land	Includes natural resources, e.g. produce from farming, or 'the gifts of nature', such as fossil fuels and renewable energy.
Labour	Includes human elements – the workers – and can refer to mental or physical labour.
Capital	Includes the equipment, machinery and tools used in the business, and also the money the owner puts into the business.
Enterprise	Includes a person (the entrepreneur) with the initial business idea, together with the other three factors of production.

At every stage of the production process, **value** is added and therefore more wealth is created. **Wealth creation** occurs because the good or service is improved during each stage of production, making that item incrementally more valuable.

Sectors of Industry

Based on the goods produced or services provided, businesses can be grouped into **sectors of industry**.

Sector of industry	Description
Primary	Businesses in this sector extract raw materials from the Earth or the oceans.
	This includes farming, forestry, mining and fishing.
Secondary	Businesses in this sector are involved in the manufacturing of products. They rely on the raw materials extracted in the primary sector.
	This includes factories and other processing plants.
Tertiary	Businesses in this sector provide a service.
	This includes retail, leisure and health.
Quaternary	Businesses in this sector provide a knowledge-based and information service.
	This includes scientific or technological research and development and education.

TOP TIP

While most countries will be engaged in all four sectors of industry, a particular country is likely to be more active in one sector over the others. It is often observed that countries move from primary to quaternary industries as they develop and become more prosperous.

TOP TIP

Some large businesses may belong to more than one sector. The multinational petrochemical giant BP extracts oil from the Earth (primary sector), processes the crude oil into petrol (secondary sector), sells to the public through its petrol stations (tertiary sector) and invests millions in research and development (quaternary sector).

Quick Fire Questions

1. Compare the role of an entrepreneur with that of a manager.
2. Describe the four factors of production.
3. How is wealth created?
4. Describe the four sectors of industry.

Sectors of the Economy 1

Private sector business organisations

Public limited companies

A public limited company (plc) is a business that is owned by shareholders who have bought shares (have shared ownership) of a business from the stock market. In return for investing in the business, the shareholder will receive a **dividend** (a percentage share of the profits). Because the number of shareholders can be very large, plcs are managed by a board of directors who have been appointed by the shareholders at the annual general meeting (AGM).

TOP TIP

Recognise the difference between sectors of industry and sectors of the economy. They are NOT the same thing.

A memorandum of association and articles of association must be produced and the plc must be government-registered as laid down in the Companies Act.

Advantages	Disadvantages
There is limited liability for shareholders.	The annual company accounts have to be published.
More sources of finance are available including debentures.	The shares can be purchased by anyone leaving the company vulnerable to a takeover.
Because of their size, they can take advantage of economies of scale.	The company has to adhere to the rules and regulations of the Companies Act.
Their size can sometimes allow them to have more power in the market.	There are significant start-up costs, which could impact on profits.

TOP TIP

Do not become confused about the words stakeholder and shareholder. A stakeholder is anyone who is interest in the continued success of the business. This includes shareholders. Shareholders are individuals who own shares in a business and therefore are part owners.

TOP TIP

Do not confuse public limited company (plcs) with public sector organisations. Plcs are private sector companies.

Franchises

A person who starts a business and provides a product or service in the name of another business is known as a **franchisee** and operates a business known as a **franchise**. The owner of the original idea who allows others to use it is known as the **franchisor**.

Advantages	Disadvantages
The franchisee is able to start a business with an established reputation and access to business experience.	The franchisee pays the franchisor.
Good ideas will be shared between all franchisees.	If one franchisee creates a bad reputation then it could impact on the whole franchise.
Growth in franchises can result in economies of scale, e.g. purchasing, transport or advertising, and even dominance of the market.	The franchisee is bound to constraints imposed by the franchisor.

Multinationals

A multinational is a business that operates in more than one country. Multinationals normally have a headquarters in one country known as the 'home' country and the other countries they operate in are known as 'host' countries.

Advantages	Disadvantages
Multinationals increase living standards by creating jobs and greater access to products and services.	Depending upon their size, multinationals can hold a great deal of power. For example, the threat of pulling out of a third world country might result in that country's government giving in to exacting demands by the multinational.
Multinationals pay taxes in the country where they earn profits.	The dominance of large foreign corporations can lead to the closure of smaller local businesses.
Multinationals can learn from other cultures and customs.	Lack of loyalty to the host country can result in multinationals pulling out when conditions change.
There are many examples of multinationals that are committed to corporate social responsibility.	Disreputable multinationals have been accused of damaging the environment in the pursuit of profit.

Quick Fire Questions

1. Describe the features of a public limited company (plc).
2. What is the name given to the share of profit received by shareholders?
3. Give one advantage and one disadvantage of a public limited company (plc).
4. Give five examples of franchises.
5. What is a multinational company?

Sample Examination Questions

1. Describe advantages of operating as a franchise.
        3 marks

2. Describe the main characteristics of a multinational corporation.
        4 marks

3. Discuss advantages and disadvantages to the host country of supporting a large foreign multinational.
        3 marks

Sectors of the Economy 2

Public sector organisations

Public sector organisations provide services to the public and are collectively owned by everyone in a country. They are controlled by the government, who will set out their priorities. Finance for public sector organisations comes mainly from taxation.

Central government	<ul><li>Central government control and provide people with essential services, such as health and defence.</li><li>The Scottish government is an example of central government. Candidates are elected (voted in) to become Members of Scottish Parliament (MSPs) or politicians.</li><li>Politicians control central government.</li></ul>
Local government	<ul><li>Local government is made up of 32 local councils, each responsible for providing services in their area. Local governments have responsibility for things like schools, roads, council housing and leisure faculties in their area. They sometimes charge for using certain facilities (e.g. swimming pools) and this, together with money direct from central government and local taxpayers, funds local government.</li><li>Elected politicians control local government and appoint managers to run the services.</li></ul>
Public corporation 	<ul><li>Public corporations provide goods and services to the public and are owned by everyone in the country. They are sometimes referred to as **nationalised** industries. The BBC is an example of a public corporation. These organisations are funded by money from the government as well as money from the public, e.g. TV Licence fees.</li><li>A Chairperson and Board of Directors manage the organisation.</li></ul>

Third sector organisations

Third sector organisations are sometimes referred to as **non-profit making** organisations and are set up to support a particular cause or activity.

Voluntary organisations	<ul><li>Voluntary organisations are managed and run by volunteers, who are willing to give up their time for no financial gain, usually because they have an interest in the organisation.</li><li>They are controlled by committees, who are usually appointed by the members of the organisation.</li></ul>

	• Funding is usually from membership fees but can also be given by local or central government, lottery funding or donations from the public. • They include the Scouts, Girl Guides or school football teams.
Charities	• Charities exist for the purpose of helping a particular cause, and usually consist of a mix of paid and voluntary workers. • They are regulated by the government who hold a register of all charities. Funding is from local or central government allowances, lottery grants and donations from public sector organisations or individual members of the public. • Charities are controlled by a Board of Trustees. • They include Oxfam, Save the Children and small local charities.
Social enterprises 	• Social enterprises have a main social or environmental aim rather than to make a profit for the owner, but – importantly – are run in a business-like way. • They provide a good or service to generate revenue for the benefit or the cause they represent, and are required to give at least half of the funds they raise to the cause they support. • People who work for social enterprises are usually paid employees but, depending upon the nature of the enterprise, they can often provide training opportunities or work experience often for those they are trying to help. • They include the *Big Issue* or the Homeless World Cup.

TOP TIP

Do not get confused with social enterprise and corporate social responsibly. A social enterprise is a third sector organisation that operates for the benefit of others. Many businesses – while pursuing profit or other goals – will operate in a socially responsible way to ensure they have a positive impact on society or minimise any negative effect on the environment.

Quick Fire Questions

Sample Examination Question

Compare features of organisations in the private, public and third sectors of the economy.

6 marks

1. Give an example of central government service.
2. Give an example of a local government service.
3. Give an example of a public corporation.
4. Compare the aims of a voluntary organisation with that of a charity.
5. Describe how a social enterprise differs from other organisations in the third sector.

Objectives

Objectives are targets or goals that an organisation sets. This provides a focus for the workforce and will often be made public, either through a **mission statement** or on the businesses' website. Objectives can act as an indicator of how successful an organisation is, by comparing aspirational objectives with actual results.

While they are generally vague statements, objectives are important in **strategic** planning, which in turn establishes **tactical** and ultimately **operational** activities. This principle can be illustrated in the form of a pyramid, which shows how each layer supports the one above.

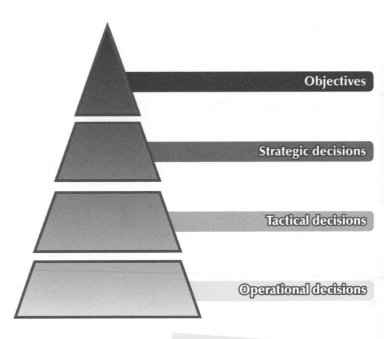

Organisations each have different objectives, and this will be made apparent when examining businesses in different sectors of the economy.

TOP TIP

The main requirement at Higher is to justify the reason for a particular objective.

Private sector objectives	Public sector objectives	Third sector objectives
<ul><li>survive</li><li>make a profit</li><li>maximise sales</li><li>become market leader</li><li>keep shareholders happy</li><li>meet managerial objectives</li></ul>	<ul><li>increase services</li><li>remain within a budget</li></ul>	<ul><li>support a cause</li><li>make the best use of money collected</li></ul>

Common objectives

- **Social responsibility:** the desire to operate in an ethical manner.
- **Positive image:** to establish trust from others in the enterprise.
- **Customer satisfaction:** to ensure continued existence of the business.
- **Satisficing:** this means to compromise, accept the best available because of constraints, e.g. lack of finance can prevent the achievement of an ultimate goal.
- **Managerial:** where the personal objectives of the managers for financial or non-financial rewards may take precedence over those of the business as a whole.

Growth

Another common objective is that of **growth**. This can take the following forms:

- **Horizontal integration:** This is where two businesses at the same stages of operation join together (for example when two banks become one).
- **Vertical integration:** This is where two businesses at different stages of the production process join together. **Backward** vertical integration is when a business buys another business that is closer to its suppliers (for example, when a supermarket buys agricultural farms to supply it with fresh fruit and vegetables). **Forward** vertical integration is when the business buys another that is closer to the customer (for example when a brewery buys a chain of pubs).
- **Diversification:** This is when two businesses providing different goods or services join forces (for example a holiday company joining forces with a car manufacturer).
- **Takeover:** This is when a large businesses takes over a smaller one. Takeovers can be **friendly**, when there is general agreement, or **hostile** where the takeover is resisted by the smaller business.
- **Merger:** When two businesses of equal size agree to amalgamate.
- **Organic growth:** This happens within a single organisation (for example, opening more branches, taking on more workers or increasing the number of products it sells, etc.).

While growth may be an objective of an organisation, the opposite might also be true.

- **Deintegration/demerger:** This occurs when two business split to become separate businesses.

TOP TIP

While a takeover and a merger are methods of growth, recognise that they are the means by which external growth takes place. When answering questions on types of growth, focus on horizontal, vertical and diversification.

Quick Fire Questions

1. Explain what business objectives are, and what a mission statement is.

2. Compare differences between the objectives of private, public and third sector organisations.

3. Describe three reasons why a business might want to grow.

4. Explain the difference between horizontal and vertical integration.

5. Describe a merger.

Sample Examination Questions

1. Discuss how a single organisation could have conflicting objectives.

      2 marks

2. Describe possible methods of growth for a public limited company.

      5 marks

3. Explain how different methods of growth can lead to increased sales or profits.

      5 marks

Internal structures 1

Organisation charts

An **organisation chart** shows how an organisation is structured. It shows:

- who has overall responsibly for the organisation
- the levels of authority and responsibility
- the lines of communication and chain of command
- the span of control and different relationships between people within the organisation
- where work can be delegated to subordinates.

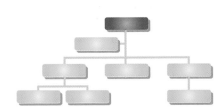

Term	Definition
Span of control	• This relates to the number of subordinates who report to a manager. • A wide span of control can be difficult to manage but a narrow span of control can be criticised as being over controlling and stifling initiative.
	Wide span of control
	Narrow span of control
Chain of command	• The line in which instructions are passed down in an organisation from one level of management to another. • A long chain of command may mean communication and decision-making takes longer, compared to a short chain of command.
Authority	• This is having the power to make decisions within an organisation. • It can denote those whom you have direct management of. • Typically, the higher up the organisation chart, the more authority an individual has.
Responsibility	• This is being answerable for decisions and the actions taken. • This normally refers to those whom a member of staff reports to within an organisation.
Delegation	• This is one of the functions of management and takes place when someone (typically higher up an organisation structure) requests a task to be completed by a subordinate. • This could be because the senior staff member does not have the time, or because the subordinate is more skilled in the task.

Grouping of activities

Organisations group their activities in a number of ways depending on several factors:

- the size of the organisation
- the technology used and availability
- the market the organisation targets
- the product, good or service, being provided
- the amount of finance available.

Grouping	Description
Functional	• People working in these departments will have similar tasks. • The departments that exist will usually be marketing, operations, human resources (people) and finance. Management Marketing — Operations — Human Resources — Finance
Product/ service	• Each department is based on a different product or service that the organisation sells. • Each department will concentrate on their specific activity, resulting in an increase in specialist product knowledge. Management Tesco plc Supermarket — Petrol stations — Banking/ finance — Mobile phone network
Customers	• Grouping is done by customer types and needs, or by different market segments. • Goods and services offered can be marketed towards each particular customer group. • In the diagram below, for a travel company, you can see that activities are grouped according to the customers' type. • Remember – different types of customers have different needs and wants. Management Family — Aged 18–30 — Couples — Older travellers
Location/ geographical	• People are grouped to focus on a particular area/region. • This is sometimes known as **place/territory** grouping. The needs of customers within each area can be specifically tailored towards them. • For example, a Scottish organisation may group its activities by region. Management East coast — West coast — Central belt — Highlands and islands

TOP TIP

Draw an organisation chart wherever you can on questions to do with grouping of activities and organisation structures.

Grouping	Description
Technology	<ul><li>A large manufacturing organisation may group its activities according to the production process and technology involved. This often occurs in large organisations with many production processes.</li><li>For example, this may include an oil and gas company operating in different sectors.</li></ul> Management — Extraction, Refinery, Distribution, Research and development
Line/staff	Organisations which have this type of grouping, group their departments according to **core** activities which support the work of other people (staff grouping) and line grouping being groups of management (e.g. managers, supervisors and so on).

Functional activities

Function	Example activities
Marketing	<ul><li>deciding on price, product, place, promotion, people, process and physical evidence for a business</li><li>taking account of the importance of people, process and physical evidence in marketing</li><li>conducting market research</li><li>devising methods of extending the product life cycle</li><li>deciding on appropriate technological resources to assist the aims of the organisations, including the use of social networking (s-commerce)</li></ul>
Operations	<ul><li>manufacturing and distributing the product</li><li>deciding which supplier of raw materials to use</li><li>ensuring the quality of the product</li><li>deciding upon the best production method</li><li>managing stock</li><li>carrying out work studies to measure production efficiency</li><li>ethical and environmental considerations, e.g. using fair trade resources</li><li>using technology in operations e.g. computer-aided design (CAD) and computer-aided manufacture (CAM)</li></ul>

Function	Example activities
Human resources (HR)	• workforce planning • recruiting and selecting staff across the organisations • using testing to aid selection • arranging training for staff, including virtual learning facilities and work-based qualifications • motivating staff and supporting positive employee relations • creating and updating HR policies • supporting the appraisal process • managing grievance and discipline procedures • keeping up-to-date with relevant employment legislation, for example the Equality Act • maintaining employee records in line with the Data Protection Act
Finance	• deciding where large businesses can get their finance • deciding on the suitability of different sources of finance for large businesses • receiving and processing requests for payments (i.e. bills) • arranging the payment of employee wages • preparing and interpreting budgets • preparing and interpreting trading, profit and loss accounts, balance sheets and cash budgets • carrying out financial analysis using ratios • presenting the financial position to management and other stakeholders • utilising technology to support the finance function of any organisations

TOP TIP

These functional areas will be dealt with later in this *Success Guide*.

Quick Fire Questions

1. What is the difference between a wide and narrow span of control?

2. Describe the terms 'chain of command', 'responsibility', 'delegate', and 'functional grouping'.

3. Explain a benefit of customer grouping.

4. Give an example of how a business might group its activities according to location/geographical grouping.

Sample Examination Questions

1. Describe the effects of increasing a manager's span of control.

   5 marks

2. Discuss the use of customer grouping for an organisation.

   4 marks

3. Compare the use of functional grouping with product grouping.

   5 marks

Internal structures 2

Types of organisation structures

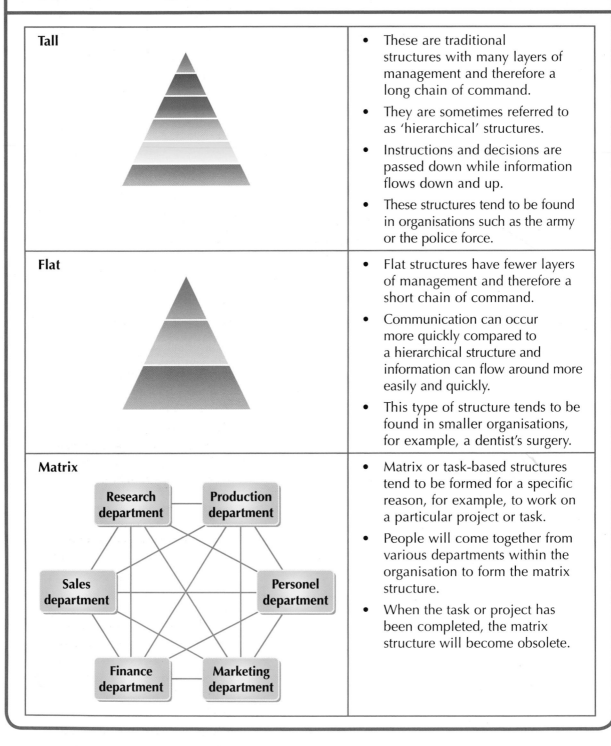

Tall	
	• These are traditional structures with many layers of management and therefore a long chain of command.
	• They are sometimes referred to as 'hierarchical' structures.
	• Instructions and decisions are passed down while information flows down and up.
	• These structures tend to be found in organisations such as the army or the police force.

Flat	
	• Flat structures have fewer layers of management and therefore a short chain of command.
	• Communication can occur more quickly compared to a hierarchical structure and information can flow around more easily and quickly.
	• This type of structure tends to be found in smaller organisations, for example, a dentist's surgery.

Matrix	
Research department, Production department, Sales department, Personel department, Finance department, Marketing department	• Matrix or task-based structures tend to be formed for a specific reason, for example, to work on a particular project or task.
	• People will come together from various departments within the organisation to form the matrix structure.
	• When the task or project has been completed, the matrix structure will become obsolete.

Entrepreneurial

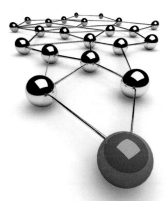

TOP TIP

Make sure you do not get mixed up with the role of the entrepreneur and that of an entrepreneurial organisation structure.

- These are commonly found in smaller organisations, when decisions are made by the owner or manager with very little input from other people – which in turn can demotivate employees.

- However, entrepreneurial structures allow for quicker decision-making.

- It is not a common structure in larger organisations because management would carry too much of a heavy workload.

- A good example of an entrepreneurial structure is that of a football managers who makes all strategic decisions during a match.

Centralised

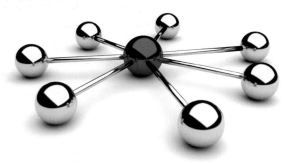

- This type of structure is associated with a hierarchical structure and decisions are made by those who are skilled at doing so.

- Decisions are made by the senior management of a company, with little involvement from staff further down the chain of command.

- It allows for a standardised approach across the organisation and avoids any conflicting approaches throughout the organisation.

Decentralised

- This type of structure is associated with a flat structure and the advantages that it brings.

- This is the opposite of a centralised organisation structure, whereby the authority (the power) to make decisions has been delegated to departments and subordinates further down the chain of command.

- Staff become empowered and this in turn will motivate them – provided they want the extra responsibility in the first place!

Relationships within organisations

Line relationships	The relationship between a subordinate and their superior. For example, a Marketing Manager has a line relationship with a Marketing Supervisor.
Lateral relationships	The relationships between people on the same level of the organisation structure. A Human Resource manager has a lateral relationship with the Operations manager.
Functional relationships	These relationships exist when one department provides support or a service to another department. The HR department, for example, has a functional relationship with other departments when they provide support during the recruitment and selection process.

Changing the structure

Organisations may decide to restructure for a number of reasons, but mainly to keep up with the changing business environment. Over recent years, there has been a decline in manufacturing in the UK because of an increase in foreign competition, changes in consumer demand and changes in government policies. Organisations must respond to external factors and – where necessary – change structure to suit the current business climate. The management of an organisation have the responsibly to ensure that the structure of the organisation meets its purpose.

Organisations can change the structure by delayering or downsizing.

Delayering

Delayering means changing from a tall, or hierarchical structure, to a flat one by removing various levels (layers) of management. Delayering allows for quicker communication, quicker decision-making and can allow the organisation to adapt to changing market conditions when necessary. Staff can feel empowered to make their own decisions and use their own initiative, which in turn can increase their motivation and productivity. This is because managers have a wider span of control. Delayering will allow the organisation to save money on the salaries of managers.

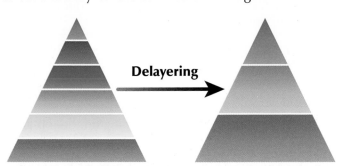

Delayering

TOP TIP

Delayering does not necessarily mean reducing the number of staff. It simply means that there are less layers of management.

Downsizing

Organisations can also change structure by downsizing. This requires the organisation to remove some of its activities from its structure, for example, a branch, factory or division. It may reduce the scale of its operations because of a decrease in demand.

Outsourcing

Some activities may be outsourced to enable the organisation to concentrate on its core activities – this could be expensive. It also means that the organisation needs to trust the outsourced organisation to deliver on time and to the standard required. Effective communication between the two organisations is crucial to the success of outsourcing.

Quick Fire Questions

1. Explain the difference between a hierarchical structure and a flat structure.
2. Why would a matrix structure be formed?
3. Where would you tend to find an entrepreneurial structure?
4. What other type of structure is a centralised structure associated with?
5. Describe a decentralised structure.
6. Why would a business decide to restructure?
7. Describe delayering, downsizing, and outsourcing.

Sample Examination Questions

1. Compare centralised and de-centralised decision-making.
   5 marks

2. Describe the main characteristics of an entrepreneurial structure.
   3 marks

3. Explain the effects of delayering on an organisation.
   4 marks

Internal factors

Internal factors are the things within a business that impact upon its success.
A business has a degree of control over internal factors.

Finance	• The funding necessary for the business to pursue its objectives. • Finance is of interest to businesses as it allows an organisation to purchase resources. Without these resources, it might not be able to compete with competitors and may have to close. • Businesses have a degree of control over finance in that they can try to obtain it from banks, debentures, government funding, share issues or the sale of an unused asset.
Employees	• This refers to the quality and skills of the workforce to ensure that the business succeeds. • Low morale or motivation can lead to poor customer relations impacting on a business' sales and profit levels. • Businesses can directly improve skills by providing on-the-job and off-the-job training.
Management	• Managers might be good or bad, depending upon their degree of training and their own personal qualities. • Poor decisions made by managers will result in bad actions that could, for example, impact on public reputation and sales. • Many organisations recognise the value of mangers and invest heavily in management training programmes and team-building events for their senior personnel.
Existing technology	• Technology is constantly improving, which can result in businesses falling behind their rivals. • Failure to embrace new ways of selling, such as through social media (known as s-commerce), will impact on a business with access to limited markets and thus fewer sales than those who do. • Businesses have fixed budgets and limited employee skills but they do have the ability to develop new technology by directly seeking additional funds or outsourcing technology to IT specialists.

Corporate culture

Another internal influence of a business is **corporate culture** or **organisational culture**. Corporate culture may be difficult to put your finger on, but never underestimate the profound impact it can have on the success or otherwise of an enterprise. It can perhaps best be described as the prevailing atmosphere or feeling within an organisation as shown by its employees.

Successful businesses have a positive culture and this is shown in the collective grit and determination of the staff to help the organisation achieve its objectives. An organisation where staff work as a team and speak in positive terms about their role, that of their co-workers and their customers is a sign of a healthy culture.

The creation of a positive culture can be a challenge for any management team. There can be no place for mistrust or suspicion. Good communication breaks down barriers between different levels of staff within a hierarchy where all employees feel listened to and valued. Changing to a flatter structure through delayering can lead to a change in culture. The goals of the organisation must be shared, perhaps through a mission statement, and team-building activities will support a sense of belonging. HR departments play a vital part in ensuring the selection of new employees who are open to or share the common principles of the organisation. Culture is visible in many organisations where staff wear similar clothes – this could be a uniform, a suit or even casual wear. What is important is that it is a common form of dress to show common values and standards.

> **TOP TIP**
>
> Corporate culture can be formal or informal. Formal corporate cultures are **created by management**. Informal cultures are **created by the workforce** and can often be regarded with suspicion.

Quick Fire Questions

1. Describe the four internal factors that impact upon the success of a business.

2. What does the term corporate culture mean?

3. Give an example of how corporate culture can be achieved.

Sample Examination Question

Describe factors an organisation should consider when trying to encourage a positive corporate culture.

5 marks

Decision making

Managers have a significant responsibility in the running of a business through the carrying out of their functional role.

Functional role	Definition
Planning	looking at future needs of the organisation
Organisation	ensuring necessary resources will be available
Commanding	instructing others in what needs to be done
Coordinating	making sure there is joined-up thinking
Controlling	overseeing developments
Delegating	entrusting tasks to others
Motivating	encouraging staff to achieve their potential

Everything a manager does involves making decisions.

Type of decisions	Description
Strategic	• long-term decisions made by senior management • they are broad or general in nature
Tactical	• medium term decisions made by senior and middle managers • these support strategic decisions and are more specific or detailed
Operational	• everyday decisions that are made by junior managers • these are everyday decisions that are unlikely to have any lasting consequence to the organisation • these are the most numerous in any organisation

TOP TIP

Decision-making can be centralised, held in the hands of a few key managers, or decentralised where it is delegated to others.

Quality decisions

The quality or effectiveness of decision-making will be based on several factors. Not all of these guarantee a good decision, but will reduce the likelihood that bad decisions will be made. These factors include:

* the actual problem that has been identified, and not simply one of the symptoms
* the experience and skills of the managers who make the decision(s)
* the reliability and relevance of the data on which the decision is made
* the amount of time available for information to be gathered and considered
* the resources available (including manpower and finance)
* the commitment of those involved to ensure that decisions are acted on.

SWOT analysis (strengths – weaknesses – opportunities – threats)

SWOT is an **analytical tool** that is used to help in strategic decision-making. The process draws together strengths, weaknesses, opportunities and threats, and is used to identify and plan a course of action to support business objectives.

Internal	**Strengths**	**Weaknesses**	**Present position**
External	**Opportunities**	**Threats**	**Future possibilities**

It is most common to set out a SWOT analysis in the form of a matrix. The analysis is broken down into four distinctive areas.

Strengths and weaknesses

- **Strengths** are internal to the business and reflect the current or present position of the organisation. Strengths identify the areas that are going well and might include: a highly qualified management team, large financial reserves, strong market share or patents and copyrights. They are areas that the business has some control over. Strengths will be used to gain a competitive advantage for the business.

- **Weaknesses** represent issues within an organisation that can cause the business to be vulnerable to competition. These include: out-of-date equipment, an unmotivated workforce and cash-flow problems. Weaknesses are areas that can be improved.

Opportunities and threats

Opportunities and **threats** represent the future position of the business. Because of the external nature of these factors, they are things that the organisation cannot directly control.

- **Opportunities** should be exploited to give the organisation a competitive edge. Examples include: deregulation of the market, developments in technology or lifestyle changes.

- **Threats** are any things that can adversely affect a business and could include potential rises in inflation, recession or potential competition.

Attempts should be made to **match** strengths with opportunities and **convert** weaknesses into strengths.

The creation of a SWOT analysis can be incredibly subjective and so it should be seen as only one analytical tool to be used in coming up with a business proposal. Other methods adopted should include desk and field market research.

TOP TIP

SWOT analysis could be the analytical tool used in your Business Management Assignment task.

Quick Fire Questions

1. Describe the seven functions of management.
2. Compare the three types of decisions made by managers.
3. Describe a factor that will influence the quality or effectiveness of a decision.
4. Give examples of one strength and one weakness which could be identified in a SWOT analysis.

External factors 1

External factors are those that influence a business but which the business has no control over. A business can simply respond to external factors to minimise or capitalise on their impact.

The external factors are easily remembered through the acronym **PESTEC**.

External Factor	Description
Political	This is the influence the government can have on an organisation. • Governments pass laws such as Health and Safety legislation, environmental targets, tax levels or minimum wage rates, which can make it more challenging for businesses to operate. • Increasing European Union membership has created opportunities for businesses to trade in a wider market without traditional restrictions such as quotas and taxes.
Economic	The state of the economy will impact on the success of any organisation. • An economic recession with high unemployment and job insecurity can be a problem for traditional businesses who will experience falling sales. • Businesses that provide 'cheaper' products can find that a recession will result in periods of growth. Consider the rise in discount supermarkets over the past few years.
Social	Changes in the population will result in changes in demand for goods and services. • Fashion and tastes change over time and this will impact on the demand for the output of organisations. • Demographic changes – changes to the population – will result in more demand, for example, for care homes or alternatively nursery care.

External Factor	Description
Technological	Emerging technology will continue to impact on the way that businesses carry out commerce. • The rise of e-commerce will put pressure on businesses to adopt this new way of interacting with customers. • Businesses that are unable to invest in new technology might find their customer base move to those who can.
Environmental	Global changes to the environment have seen businesses respond differently to these challenges. • Industries involved in the tertiary sector of industry are often hostage to changes in the environment. Consider the impact that a particular wet summer will have on farming. • Firms who are socially responsible, caring for the environment (for example, through recycling), can find that an added benefit of this action is an increased interest in their product.
Competition	This is perhaps one of the simplest external factors to appreciate. • When a close competitor lowers prices, improves the product, increases promotion, changes distribution methods, then others are likely to have to follow or lose customers. • When a competitor exits the market after voluntary restructuring, or because of government legislation to limit monopolies, there are opportunities for the rivals to increase their market share.

> **TOP TIP**
>
> External factors can have negative or positive impacts on an organisation.

Quick Fire Questions

Sample Examination Question

Discuss the impact that political factors can have on an organisation.   **4 marks**

1. Give an example of a political factor that could impact on the activities of a business.

2. Suggest an economic factor that can impact on the success of a business.

3. What social changes have there been that will influence demand?

4. Can you think of any changes in technology that change the way businesses operate?

5. How can a business become more socially responsible?

External factors 2

Government intervention

The global nature of business has resulted in an increased awareness of how government intervention, often in the form of laws, can impact on the way businesses achieve their objectives. Such actions are designed to support the interests of consumers by protecting businesses, and yet prevent such businesses becoming so powerful that they act in ways detrimental to the public good.

Government intervention is an external impact on business, which we have learned is the 'P' or political factor from PESTEC, but it is worth considering this influence under two subheadings: Economic policy and Competition policy.

Economic policy

Economic policy is how government institutions influence business activity. It covers the setting of interest rates, controlling inflation and government spending.

Despite being in different countries, many government institutions are connected and work together to globally influence the world economy.

Economic policy	Influence on objectives
Banks across the world have restricted lending following a banking crisis that started with an American bank called Lehman Brothers.	Some businesses have found it difficult to secure funds for growth.
Budget problems in many European countries have led the EU to impose austerity packages to curb government spending.	This has restricted the ability of businesses to earn money from selling goods and services to the Public Sector.

Economic policy	Influence on objectives
Government policy is to keep inflation (rises in prices) to a minimum. They have done this through restricting pay deals in the Public Sector and reducing public spending and borrowing.	Less spending has led to a fall in demand for goods and services.
The Bank of England is influential in setting interest rates across other banks. The Bank of England has kept interest rates historically low.	Lower interest rates encourage people to spend, not save. This encourages economic growth.
Quantitative easing (QE) is when the government pumps money into the economy.	This provides 'new' money, which is passed on, thus stimulating consumer spending and economic growth.
Governments provide state aid if there is a case that such funding is likely to result in the long-term viability of the business.	Several industries have been dependent upon state subsidies for their survival.

Economic policies are influenced by the directives of national and international bodies, including the European Parliament, and institutions like the International Monitory Fund (the World Bank), the European Central Bank and the Bank of England.

Competition policy

Competition is generally regarding as **a good thing** across the world as it tends to make businesses more competitive, which benefits consumers.

Competition policy	Influence on objectives
The European Union single market has removed trade barriers between member states.	This has opened up markets to many Scottish businesses, increasing sales but equally made them vulnerable to competition from abroad.
Antitrust and cartels are private agreements between businesses that artificially set prices higher than they should be. This practice is against the law and businesses found colluding in this way will be fined and individuals could be sent to prison.	Fixing prices artificially high will allow business to earn abnormal profits.
The government has opened up the market in areas that previously might have been a monopoly. This has happened with the energy industry and most recently with postal services.	It is argued that this should lead to falling prices for the consumer and business opportunities for entrepreneurs.
Government agencies will investigate takeover and mergers and can prevent vertical or horizontal growth taking place if the new joint business would be against general public interest.	A merger or a takeover can be blocked and this will impact on the growth objective of a business.

The official regulators of competition include the Office of Fair Trading, the UK Competition and Markets Authority (CMA) and the European Union Competition Commission.

TOP TIP

In PESTEC, Economic policy and Competition policy are part of P (Political) and not E (Economic) or C (Competition).

Quick Fire Questions

1. What impact will tighter lending controls by banks have on a business?

2. How does the adoption of an austerity package reduce demand for goods and services?

3. Suggest an impact of low interest rates on the economy.

4. Does QE increase or decrease economic growth?

Sample Examination Question

Discuss the role Competition policy has in achieving business objectives.

4 marks

Stakeholders

A stakeholder is anyone who has an interest in the continued survival of the business. The table below provides examples – **it is not exhaustive**. At Higher level the emphasis is likely to be on *interdependence* and *conflict*.

Stakeholder	Interest	Influence	Impact	Interdependence	Conflict
Owner/ Shareholders	They want a return on investment in the form of dividends.	They vote at AGM on who to appoint to the Board of Directors.	Panic selling of shares can cause the share price to fall, resulting in lower funds from new share issues.	The shareholders are dependent upon the management to make the most profitable decision for the business.	Shareholders might be interested in quick returns and resist funds being reinvested in the business.
Management	They can look for a certain amount of experience, recognition or a bonus.	They make the strategic and tactical decisions.	Bad decisions will result in bad actions, such as a bad advertising campaign.	A manager is only as good as their team. Poor workers will let a manager down.	The management want the workforce to work hard, but this is not always what employees want.
Employees	They want high wages and good conditions of service.	A helpful employee will result in happy customers.	Happy customers will mean sales and profits.	Employees need to be directed and this is where they need managers.	Employees might want to suit themselves and reduce opening hours – this will conflict with customers.
Customers	They want value for money.	They can decide to take their custom elsewhere.	This could result in the business closing.	Customers rely on the employee to satisfy needs.	Demands of customers for low prices might conflict with the aim of shareholders for high profits.
Government	Governments want to see most businesses succeed to reduce unemployment – increasing taxes and reducing benefit payments.	They can provide grants or restrict planning permission.	Failure to give a grant or planning permission could result in a business failing to achieve its objective of growth.	Government is elected by the electorate from the local community.	Government representatives often walk a tightrope between the wishes of businesses to grow and local communities who want to restrict noise pollution.

GOVERNMENT GRANT

Stakeholder	Interest	Influence	Impact	Interdependence	Conflict
Local community	Businesses lead to general prosperity in a local community and have been shown to reduce crime rates.	They can protest if a business is causing increased road pollution.	Bad publicity can lead to a fall in sales or withdrawal of government support, leading to financial problems.	The local community needs the support of the government to provide incentives to keep businesses in an area.	The local community sometimes want a status quo to exist, while businesses often look for restructuring, for example the closure of a factory.
Suppliers	They rely on fellow businesses for their existence.	Suppliers set prices and credit conditions.	Short credit terms can lead to cash flow problems for businesses.	While a customer deals directly with a business it ultimately relies on that business' ability to get materials from the supplier.	The manager wants to get the cheapest price from the supplier in order to achieve the highest profit, while the supplier in turn wants to earn the highest profit by charging the highest prices.
Pressure groups	While still wanting the business to continue, they might wish to change the way it operates, for example to become more environmentally friendly.	Pressure groups can lobby governments to put pressure on businesses to change the way they carry out their activities.	Protesting and raising public awareness of an issue can result in falling share price or sales.	To have any impact on the businesses, they must have the support of the government and or the local community.	Becoming environmentally responsible can be costly and result in a fall in profits: both are likely to upset shareholders who are looking for a high dividend.

TOP TIP

'Impact' is the stage beyond 'influence'.

Conflict resolution

The final column in the table on the previous two pages, provides examples of conflict that can exist between stakeholders. Resolution of such conflict, or disagreement, can be resolved through:

- the Stakeholder with the greatest **influence** getting their own way
- the Stakeholder with the greatest **impact** getting their way by holding the other side to ransom

- a compromise between the conflicting stakeholders where each side gives in a bit – this recognises **interdependence**
- the involvement of external agencies to negotiate or impose a solution, for example, The Advisory, Conciliation and Arbitration Service (ACAS) or the local Planning Authority.

> **TOP TIP**
>
> Competitors are NOT stakeholders because they do not want the other businesses to succeed.

Quick Fire Questions

1. Suggest stakeholders for an organisation of your choice.
2. Explain the interdependence of two stakeholders.
3. Explain the conflict between two stakeholders.
4. Discuss how the conflict identified above may be resolved.

Recruitment

Recruitment is the process of getting potential candidates to apply for a job vacancy.

Recruitment methods

Internal recruitment involves appointing existing employees to new positions within the business – this includes promotion.

External recruitment involves appointing new employees from outwith the business. Jobs are advertised externally and anyone can apply.

Analysis of recruitment methods

	Advantages	Disadvantages
Internal recruitment	• There are no external advertising fees. • Staff are already known to the business. • Less training is required as existing staff already know the organisation.	• Some staff may feel 'passed over' when another member of staff is promoted. • There is no 'fresh blood' brought into the organisation with new ideas. • Higher salaries may have to be paid.
External recruitment	• There is a wider range of applicants with new ideas. • It may be quicker to move the business along in terms of growth and expansion. • If employees have relevant experience they may not need as much training.	• Costs of advertising externally or using an agency. • Existing staff may feel aggrieved that they have not been considered. • New employees may take a long time to become familiar with the organisation.

Stages of the recruitment process

Each business or organisation will go through a number of stages in order to recruit the best employee.

1. Identify a job vacancy – making sure that the job exists.

2. Conduct a job analysis – setting out in detail what the job involves.

3. Prepare a job description – clarifying the duties, responsibilities, salary, working conditions of the job.

4. Prepare a person specification – clarifying the essential skills and qualities, and the desirable skills, qualities and any other characteristics.

5. Advertise the vacancy, internally and externally – jobs can be advertised in a variety of places, usually newspapers/magazines, websites and the job centre.

6. Send out application forms and/or ask for a CV (curriculum vitae).

TOP TIP

It is important to know the difference between a job description, which is about the job itself, and a person specification, which is about the type of person the business is looking for to fill the job.

Recruitment agencies

A **recruitment agency** may be used to find a suitable candidate for the vacancy. The agency can filter applications and CVs, and conduct the assessments and interviews of candidates. The agency will often already have a list of candidates that they can match against the person specification. The business will therefore save time and money by avoiding long lists of candidates who do not meet the criteria. Once the agency has selected the most suitable candidates, the business can be involved in the final interviews.

Stages in workforce planning

Businesses have to plan their workforce requirements in order to meet their strategic objectives. Having the right balance of employees with different skills, knowledge, qualifications and abilities is challenging and constantly changing. The four stages involved in workforce planning are as follows.

1. Know the strategic business objectives

The business must know what it is aiming to do in terms of developing new products and the timescales. For example, will they need new designers this year or next year? Are they aiming to expand by mergers or takeovers?

2. Analyse the labour market

The business has to know what is available in terms of the workforce. Are they going to be able to recruit staff who are qualified in their specialist area? For example, sometimes there are shortages of engineers, software engineers, teachers, etc. Analysing the labour market involves gathering information about potential employees from sources such as recruitment agencies, LinkedIn (business website), university graduates and school leavers. Businesses have to know what is available. Many businesses have partnerships with universities in order to recruit specialist labour.

3. Analyse the business demand

Once the business knows what is available in terms of the potential workforce, they can gather market research information to gauge the demand for their products and services in the future. This will give them an idea of how many employees they will need and also the qualities, skills and experience they should have.

4. Analyse the existing workforce

The business will also have to closely examine their current workforce.

- How many employees have to be re-trained?
- How many employees are due to retire soon?
- How many employees are likely to seek new jobs elsewhere?
- How are these employees going to be replaced?
- How are employees retained if they have the necessary skills and experience?

Once all these steps have been followed, the business will be able to put together a workforce plan to ensure that there are no gaps in the workforce requirements in the future.

> **TOP TIP**
>
> Workforce planning is a detailed and comprehensive process, which has to be updated constantly in order to make sure that employees are in the right place, at the right time, with the right skills.

Quick Fire Questions

1. Explain what workforce planning is and how a business would carry it out.
2. Distinguish between internal and external recruitment.
3. Explain the difference between a job description and a person specification.
4. Name three places that job vacancies can be advertised.
5. Outline how a recruitment agency could be used.

> **Sample Examination Question**
>
> Describe five stages of the recruitment process used by most organisations.
>
> **5 marks**

Selection of employees

The selection process

Once all the applications and CVs have been received from candidates, the selection process begins to find the best person to fill the job vacancy. In the first instance, the applications have to be cross-checked with the person specification to ensure that the candidates meet all the criteria. Those who do not will be discarded at this point. The business then has to decide the best way in which to select the best candidate. There are different methods of selection and there is also the possibility of using an assessment centre.

Selection methods

Interview

Candidates will be invited for an interview and an interview panel will be formed. During the interview each panel member will assess the candidate's answers to a set list of questions and their overall performance. After interviewing all the candidates, the panel will assess the best performance and fit for the business.

Presentation

Candidates may be asked to give a presentation to the panel. This could involve using a flip chart, or a computer and data projector. The topic for the presentation would usually be given to the candidates in advance.

Role play

Candidates may be asked to take part in a scenario that shows how they react in different situations, such as dealing with a difficult customer. The role play is designed to show the strengths, weaknesses and personality of the candidates.

Group interviews

Candidates may be asked to take part in a group interview. This allows the business to see who emerges as a natural leader, but also to see how candidates interact with one another.

Team-building tasks

Candidates may be asked to work as part of a team to solve a particular problem. They would be expected to work together to come up with an acceptable solution. This tests candidates' team-working skills, such as listening, giving instructions, following instructions and interpersonal skills.

TOP TIP

Remember the difference between recruitment and selection. Recruitment stops at the point where candidates have all applied for the job. Selection begins when they start to narrow down the candidates using selection methods.

Psychometric testing

Psychometric tests fall into two main categories: **personality questionnaires**, which try to measure aspects of your personality, and **aptitude tests**, which try to measure your intellectual and reasoning abilities.

Personality tests ask you about your thoughts, feelings and your behaviour in a variety of situations. The tests can be tailored to suit the business, for example, supermarkets would ask questions about dealing with customers, whereas medical tests would ask about dealing with patients. The results of personality tests enable the business to match up personalities with specific jobs.

Aptitude tests cover a range of areas, such as literacy, numeracy, problem-solving and reasoning. Again the tests can be tailored to suit the business, for example, an engineering business would be interested in numeracy and problem-solving. The results of the tests are more specific than personality tests, as there are likely to be more questions that have a definite answer. The results of these tests are therefore very important in selecting candidates.

Assessment centres

The use of assessment centres has grown in recent years, with some businesses using them to carry out the last stage of the selection process. Assessment centres should not be confused with recruitment agencies, who can provide all stages in the recruitment and selection process.

The assessment centre can be based in the business itself or in a hotel, university, or recruitment agency. It is usually somewhere with plenty of space and a relaxing environment. The activities that candidates will undertake can involve:

- group exercises
- in-tray exercises
- presentations
- case studies
- psychometric testing
- social activities, such as lunch and coffee breaks.

The activities can take place over a morning, a full day or maybe even two days, depending on the level of job. After all the activities have been completed, the business or recruiters have a very comprehensive picture of the skills, abilities and personality of the candidates being assessed. They can therefore make very reliable judgments about the best candidate for the job.

Probationary periods

Once candidates have been appointed, the business may wish to stipulate that their appointment is for a trial period or a **probationary period**. This means that the candidate has to demonstrate an acceptable level of performance during this time before they will be appointed permanently. This allows the business to ensure that at the end of this period they have the best candidate for the job with a proven track record.

Quick Fire Questions

1. Outline two methods of selecting candidates.
2. Explain the difference between recruitment and selection.
3. What are the advantages of using team-building and group discussion to select candidates?
4. Outline how a psychometric test measures personality and aptitude.
5. Name three activities that candidates might undertake in an assessment centre.
6. What is a trial or probationary period?

Sample Examination Questions

1. Describe a selection process that an organisation could use to ensure it employs the best workers.
   4 marks

2. Describe the benefits to an organisation of using interviews prior to appointing a new employee.
   3 marks

3. Describe and justify **three** forms of testing (other than interviews) in the selection process. (A different justification should be used each time.)
   6 marks

Training and development

Types of training

- **On-the-job training** is carried out in the work place. It is undertaken by employees to improve their knowledge, skills and performance at work.
- **Off-the-job training** is carried out away from the work place. It can be undertaken at college, university, training centres or other venues. It may involve additional qualifications. The training is usually delivered by experts in their field.
- **Induction training** is usually carried out in the work place. It is offered to new employees and can include information about the wider business environment as well as specific training about the new job. Induction training usually also involves health and safety issues, arrangements for signing in and out, holidays, sickness, social arrangements etc.

TOP TIP

Be clear about the difference between types and methods of training.

Methods of training

Whichever type of training is undertaken, it can be delivered in a variety of ways.

- **Lectures** are often used with off-the-job training to reach large numbers of people at the same time. They are a useful way of giving information.
- **Role playing and simulation** enable employees to react in a realistic way to solving customer problems or dealing with other colleagues. Employees are asked to 'play out' a scenario in order to learn from this.
- **Job rotation** involves moving an employee through a series of jobs so they can get a good feel for the tasks that are associated with different roles.
- **Apprenticeships** are especially appropriate for jobs requiring production skills, for example, plumbing, engineering, etc. However, they are also used now for young employees in administration and business roles.
- **Multimedia** training can take a variety of different forms, such as DVDs, PowerPoint presentations, films, computer simulations, etc. Many of these can be undertaken by the employee in their own time away from work.

Benefits of training

All forms of training – no matter where or when they take place – contribute to the business or organisation achieving their strategic objectives. Training leads to greater efficiency and effectiveness, which in turn means that the business can be more competitive in the market place.

The table below summarises the benefits of training.

Employer	Employee
Higher skilled more effective employees leads to reductions in customer complaints.	Increased skills and knowledge therefore greater effectiveness in their job.
Higher skilled more effective employees leads to reductions in absenteeism and staff turnover.	Increased morale and motivation at work therefore higher productivity.
Higher skilled more effective employees will be ambitious and will apply for vacancies, therefore reducing the skills gap.	Increased confidence and possibility of promotion or salary increases based on performance.

Virtual learning environments (VLE)

Staff training can now take place through the medium of a VLE. A VLE can be set up by the business as a web-based resource for employees to access from home or from work. It operates like a classroom and the learner can be put in touch with a trainer, teacher or supervisor to help them with their learning. Notes, resources, videos, assessments are all loaded onto the system and the employee can undertake reading and assessment, as and when they are ready. There is usually some form of electronic communication available, such as a chat facility, bulletin board or email list.

The disadvantages and benefits of a VLE are shown in the table below.

Advantages	Disadvantages
Employees do not have to lose time away from their jobs in order to be trained.	Finance required for computers and other equipment.
Travel costs, and the costs of paying lecturers and trainers, are reduced.	Some employees do not like to learn in a VLE – they may be more comfortable learning in a more traditional way.
Employees will feel more motivated if they have training opportunities, and will produce better quality work as their skills improve.	If the Internet or network system is down employees are unable to access the VLE, which can lead to delays in completing their training.

Professional development training schemes

Business and organisations offer training schemes so that employees can develop their skills and knowledge through work. Training schemes do not necessarily lead to formal qualifications, but they provide the employee with skills and knowledge needed for that particular job. Examples of training schemes are graduate training schemes (for university leavers) and vocational training (for particular jobs and businesses).

Professional development work-based qualifications

Many business sectors allow employees to work and study for qualifications at the same time. There are many examples from professional occupations, such as:

- Health
- Accountancy
- Business
- Customer Care
- Health and Safety
- ICT
- Horticulture.

Employees are usually taken on with the agreement that they will study for their qualifications at the same time. The level of qualification can vary, for example apprenticeships are structured training programmes that lead to qualifications relevant to the industry, for example, plumbing, joinery, etc. Other qualifications can be at degree-level, for example, accountancy, ICT. The employee may attend college or university at various times – away from the work place or in the evenings.

> ### TOP TIP
> Make sure if you are asked about the benefits of training that you make it clear whether the benefits are for the employer or the employee.

Quick Fire Questions

1. Name three types of training.
2. Outline two methods of training.
3. Outline two benefits of training for the employer.
4. Give two examples of professional development training schemes.
5. Outline two costs and two benefits of a VLE.

Sample Examination Questions

1. Explain the advantages of staff training for an organisation.
   4 marks

2. Describe the costs of staff training.
   4 marks

Motivation and leadership

Theories of motivation

Employees want to feel motivated at work in order to feel satisfied with their jobs. Employers also want to get the best out of their employees. There are a number of theories that have been put forward over a period of time, which outline how this can be achieved.

Motivation theory	Details
Taylor's theory (Frederick Winslow Taylor)	This theory states that employees are only interested in money and have to be treated in such a way that they are controlled and directed to do the tasks that managers want them to do. Taylor claimed that work should be broken down into a series of small repetitive tasks that workers would be able to do quite easily. While this did increase productivity, employees soon became bored with repetitive tasks and being treated like machines rather than people.
Mayo's theory (Eric Mayo)	Mayo believed that employees needed more than just money at work. He claimed that employees needed to interact with each other and with management in order to be happy at work. His theory was based on better communication between managers and workers, greater management involvement and working in teams. All of this improved motivation and productivity.
Maslow's theory (Abraham Maslow)	Maslow's theory was more complex, stating that employees had five levels of human needs to be met at work. These needs were in a hierarchy – the lowest in the hierarchy had to be met first before moving to the next level (see diagram).

Self actualisation

Esteem Needs
Self-esteem
Recognition
Status

Social needs
Sense of belonging
Love

Safety needs
Security
Protection

Physiological needs
Hunger
Thirst

Motivation theory	Details
Herzberg's theory (Frederick Herzberg)	Herzberg believed that there were two factors which affect employees in the work place: i) **motivators**, which motivate employees, such as how interesting the work is; ii) **hygiene factors**, which do not motivate employees, but would de-motivate them if they were not present, e.g. safe working conditions. Herzberg also believed that the nature of the job should be enhanced by strategies such as job enrichment, job enlargement and empowering employees to feel more responsible.

Motivating staff – leadership styles

It is important that business owners and managers lead and motivate their staff in order to get the best from them. Motivation comes in a variety of ways – through financial and non-financial rewards, but also through proper leadership and employees feeling a sense of pride and being valued. So, depending on the type of leadership, employees may be motivated or they may lack motivation. Business leaders do not all fit neatly into any one particular category, but a useful analysis of leadership styles is outlined below.

Leadership style	Characteristics
Autocratic	<ul><li>gives instructions and orders without negotiation or discussion</li><li>no real input from employees</li><li>employees are not encouraged to use their initiative</li><li>can lead to high staff turnover</li><li>good system for the army, where orders are given to be followed</li></ul>
Democratic	<ul><li>managers consult with employees before making decisions</li><li>employees feel included and therefore are more motivated</li><li>employees can use their initiative</li><li>managers may delegate authority to others to make decisions</li><li>less staff turnover, as staff are happy at work</li><li>can lead to delays in decision-making as there are more people involved</li></ul>
Laissez-faire	<ul><li>managers do not give clear direction to employees as they are 'hands off' and allow employees to make their own decisions</li><li>works well if employees are capable of making their own decisions</li><li>can be ineffective if employees are inexperienced, and can lead to problems with missing deadlines</li></ul>

Financial rewards

Employees are expected to be motivated by pay, as that is the reason why most people go to work. There are different methods of payment.

- **Time rates:** Employees are paid by the hour. The government has set a minimum hourly wage, which must be paid to all employees.
- **Piece rates:** Employees are paid according to the amount they produce. This has to be measured in some way. If employees work harder and produce more, they can earn more.
- **Wage/salary (flat rate):** Employees are paid an agreed wage or salary per week or per month for doing their job.
- **Overtime:** Hours worked beyond the normal working day or week. Overtime is often paid at above the employee's normal rate.
- **Bonus:** Bonuses are paid for a variety of reasons, over and above the normal wage or salary.

Non-financial rewards

There are other ways of rewarding or motivating employees that do not involve direct payments.

- **Company car:** A car is given to the employee to use for work, but it can also be used for their own purposes.
- **Pension/insurance:** Employees can join the company pension scheme or enjoy reduced rates for life insurance.
- **Luncheon vouchers/subsidised canteen:** This reduces the cost of employee lunches each day.
- **Staff discount:** Giving cost savings for employees on company products.
- **Child care vouchers/crèche schemes:** These help employees with expensive childcare costs.

> **TOP TIP**
>
> Make sure you can distinguish between financial and non-financial rewards and how they motivate employees

Quick Fire Questions

1. Outline two theories of motivating employees.
2. Outline the characteristics of a democratic leader.
3. Explain the difference between financial and non-financial rewards.
4. How do rewards help to motivate employees?
5. Outline two financial and two non-financial rewards.

Sample Examination Questions

1. Discuss methods that an organisation could use to ensure their staff stay motivated.

   4 marks

2. Compare the use of 'time rate' with 'piece rate' for paying employees.

   3 marks

3. Describe other employee payment systems that could be used by an organisations.

   4 marks

Employee relations 1

Employee relations involves encouraging and motivating staff to develop and perform to their potential in their job. It also involves communicating, negotiating and bargaining with staff on a more official basis, through trade unions and works councils. Employee relations can have a positive effect on the success of the business, as staff work well and customers are happy. However, employee relations can also have a negative effect on the success of the business if employees are unhappy and industrial action is being undertaken. Employee relations therefore often involves negotiating with trade unions, when appropriate, to secure positive outcomes.

Motivation of staff

Businesses try to keep their employees motivated in other ways too – how depends on the type and size of business. A number of these are listed below.

- **Works council:** A committee made up of employees and managers, to enable the employees to be consulted and involved in the decision-making process of the business.

- **Team-working:** Employees are given the opportunity to work with others in teams or on specific projects. They share decision-making, successes and failures. They learn from each other and build trust and respect.

- **Staff training:** As previously outlined, staff training and development leads to increased efficiency and a higher rate of staff retention.

- **Communication:** Employees value giving their opinions and being listened to. But equally, they do not usually have a difficulty with following instructions provided they are kept informed of decisions and the reasons why they have been made. Many employees say they want transparency in communication.

- **Support systems:** Many businesses and organisations have a separate HR department to provide a range of support to employees. This can take the form of counselling for stress or bereavement. There may be absence management procedures, where employees are encouraged to take part in 'return to work' interviews or a 'phased' return to work after a long absence. They may offer a range of 'family friendly' policies, such as flexible working or working from home.

- **Quality circles:** These groups of volunteer employees discuss how to improve the business. They can be responsible for implementing suggestions on how improvements can be made.

- **Employee of the month and achievement awards:** Many businesses operate schemes whereby employees can receive awards, bonuses or recognition for their role in the business. These can be competition-type events or based on feedback from customers and colleagues.

- **The working environment:** Many businesses have recognised the importance of a positive working environment.
    - They provide areas for relaxation or playing games.
    - Some offer reduced price or free gym membership.
    - Others employ professionals to help with stress management or alternative therapies, such as reflexology.
    - Other arrangements include team-building days out and social events.

- **Good career structure:** Employees may be more motivated when they can move up the career ladder and apply for promoted posts within the business or organisation.

- **Employee appraisals:** An appraisal system can be a focus for employees to work towards a bonus or promotion, or to request training and development in order to progress in their job.

TOP TIP

Not every business can offer all of these methods of motivation, but all businesses should try and offer something extra to motivate their employees.

Quick Fire Questions

1. Explain the term employee relations.
2. Outline two support systems that can be put in place for employees.
3. Explain how the working environment can help employees stay motivated.
4. What is the purpose of employee appraisals?
5. What would be the result if a business did not try and motivate their employees?

Sample Examination Questions

1. Appraisal has identified poor performance for a member of staff. Describe the actions that a manager could take to improve the employee's performance.
   6 marks

2. Explain the effects that poor employee relations could have on an organisation.
   4 marks

Employee relations 2

Trade unions

A trade union is an organisation that employees can join for support: usually to help them negotiate better pay and conditions. A trade union will advise its members, help resolve disputes with employers and offer additional benefits such as financial services and legal advice.

Industrial action

There are different methods of industrial action – some more damaging than others. All forms of industrial action penalise the business, but employees can also suffer through loss of earnings.

- **Strike:** Employees refuse to go to work but do not get paid.
- **Overtime ban:** Employees refuse to work overtime and lose pay.
- **Sit-in:** Employees occupy the premises and normal work cannot take place.
- **Work to rule:** Employees only do exactly what their contract states. Goodwill is damaged and some overtime payments may be lost.
- **Go slow:** Employees still carry out their duties but do so more slowly or with reduced productivity.

TOP TIP

There can be positive benefits from industrial action, for example, introducing new procedures that all employees will follow and be happy with.

ACAS

When industrial disputes cannot be resolved, businesses can ask for direct help from an organisation called ACAS. ACAS provides information, advice, training, conciliation and other services to help prevent or resolve workplace problems.

Their overall aim is to improve employee relations and to help disputes from arising in the first place or escalating after they have begun. Often ACAS provides **arbitration**, where both sides in the dispute ask for an agreement to be reached that they can both adhere to.

Legislation

There are a number of laws that have to be followed by both employers and employees.
e laws are designed to make the working environment safe and to ensure that employees
reated fairly in the work place.

Health and Safety at Work Act 1974

This law outlines the responsibilities of both employers and employees in relation to health and safety at work. Employers have a duty to:

- provide and maintain safety equipment and safe systems of work
- ensure materials used are properly stored, handled, used and transported
- provide information, training, instruction and supervision
- provide a safe place of employment, e.g. fire extinguishers, protective clothing
- appoint health and safety representatives.

If employees felt that their employer was not carrying out their duties properly in terms of the law, they can complain to the Health and Safety Executive (HSE) or to their trade union representative. Employees will be at risk if they are not properly trained or do not have proper equipment safety equipment. Employees have a duty to:

- take reasonable care of the health and safety of themselves, and of others who may be affected by what they do/do not do
- co-operate with the employer on health and safety matters.

The Equality Act 2010

The Equality Act 2010 bans unfair treatment and helps achieve equal opportunities in the workplace and in wider society. It brings together previous Acts that deal with discrimination, and makes it unlawful to discriminate against anyone on the grounds of sex, race, marital status, religion and belief, disability, sexual orientation or pregnancy.

A business or organisation has to make sure that when recruiting they do not have any bias or prejudice in their job descriptions or person specifications. They must ensure that candidates are not disadvantaged during recruitment and selection procedures, for example, with limited access for wheelchairs to the building. They must provide all the necessary support for employees to do their job with discrimination.

The Minimum Wage Act 1998

This law was passed to ensure that employees received a minimum wage in order to avoid poverty and exploitation. The minimum wage varies, depending on the age of the employee. The rate is set by the government and increases are applied each year.

Quick Fire Questions

1. What is the purpose of a trade union?
2. Outline two methods of industrial action.
3. Describe two duties of employers under the Health and Safety at Work Act.
4. What are the purposes of the Equality Act 2010 and the Minimum Wage Act?

Sample Examination Questions

1. Describe the main features of the Equality Act 2010.
         3 marks

2. The introduction of new technology may cause unrest in the workplace. Describe four forms of industrial action.
         4 marks

Management of finance

The role and importance of the finance function

All organisations depend upon the effective management of finance for their very survival and the achievement of other objectives. No study of business management would be complete without a detailed knowledge of the function of finance within organisations. The finance department carries out the following activities.

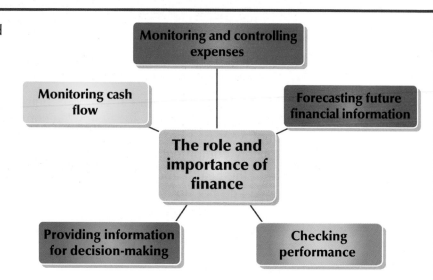

Monitoring and controlling expenses

All expenses must be carefully tracked to ensure that the organisation does not end up in financial difficulty. This will ensure that: businesses in the private sector have a chance to achieve the objective of profit maximisation; organisations in the public sector break-even; and third sector organisations generate sufficient funds to support the causes for which they were established.

Monitoring and controlling finances requires the preparation of budgets. A budget acts as both a guide and a constraint when spending money.

The finance department of a business plays a vital role in establishing wage rates for its employees and any negotiation with trade unions.

Monitoring cash flow

'Liquidity' is the term given to the flow of funds within an organisation. The absence of enough funds to pay for debts as they are due – including debts to HM Revenue & Customs (HMRC) – can lead to the closure and liquidation of an otherwise profitable business.

Monitoring cash flow is done through the preparation of cash budgets, and will regularly require securing additional funds to prevent negative cash flow.

Forecasting future financial information

The job of the finance team is to calculate what-if scenarios. This means that they are expected to estimate revenue and expenditure for various options to support strategic planning.

This is a highly skilled activity and often requires a retrospective look at finances in order to make future predictions.

Checking performance

There are well established accounting statements and procedures, including ratio analysis (see pages 68–71), which are used to look at how well an organisation is performing financially.

It is the function of the finance section to produce final accounts and for most large organisations, including plcs, there is a legal requirement that these should be made available to the general public.

Providing information for decision-making

An internal constraint for a business is the availability of suitable sources of finance. Strategic planning will have to take account of funding, and the role of the finance department is to ensure that managers are aware of the financial constraints or opportunities within the organisation.

This might require the finance department to propose financial solutions in the form of savings or to suggest sources of additional funding.

Users of financial information

There are several different groups of people who can make use of a company's financial information as detailed in the table below:

Stakeholder	Interest in financial information	
Employees	<ul><li>They need to see if their employer is paying a fair wage.</li><li>They need to see if the business can afford better working conditions.</li><li>They need to judge the security of their job.</li></ul>	Employees Salaries
Government agencies	<ul><li>They need to ensure that correct rates of tax are being paid (HMRC). Multinational companies might try to avoid paying tax in one country where corporation tax is high and declare profits in a country where the tax rate is lower. Governments will need to ensure that this is legal.</li><li>They need to prevent companies taking advantage of a monopoly position, lack of competition, or behaving in an unreasonable way (Competition Commission).</li></ul>	Consulting Taxes

Stakeholder	Interest in financial information
Government agencies (continued)	• In the case of multinational companies, they need to ensure that businesses are not making unreasonable profits by exploiting their workforce or the environment in less-developed countries. • They need to see if the government can help businesses that are genuinely in need of financial support or tax breaks. • They need to check that third sector organisations are not abusing their position and are really supporting the causes they have set out to help. • They need to see if they provide value for (tax-payers') money in public sector organisations and identify areas for savings.
Owners/ shareholders	• They need to make sure there is a fair return on their investment. • They need to judge how successful the management are. • They need to decide if they should continue to invest.
Lenders	• They need to judge if the business can pay back borrowed money.
Suppliers	• They need to decide on the degree of credit to give. (*Credit terms are the period of time before a customer needs to pay for goods purchased from them.*)
General public	• They need to see how secure the organisation is and whether it will continue in the future. • They need to check the amount spent on social responsibility.

Quick Fire Questions

1. In your own words, summarise the role and importance of the finance function. Use the following headings: 'Monitoring and controlling of expenses', 'Forecasting future financial information', 'Checking performance', 'Providing information for decision-making', 'Monitoring cash flow'.

2. Explain why the following would be interested in the financial information of a business: an employee, an owner, a shareholder, the general public, a supplier.

3. Name a government agency that scrutinise the accounts of a business.

4. Suggest a reason why a lender would look at the financial position of a company before lending to them.

Cash budgets

A cash budget is a prediction of the flow of cash in and out of an organisation. They are normally shown for a quarter of a year (3 months). Managers use cash budgets to identify periods when cash-flow might be a problem and therefore enable them to take correction actions, such as applying for a loan or delaying capital expenditure. Cash budgets can also be used to suggest periods where there will be spare funds that can be put to some positive use.

As the name suggests, cash budgets look at cash coming in and going out of the organisation. Most businesses will conduct transactions on credit – delaying payment until some future date. Credit payments will only be recorded in a cash budget at the point it is predicted that cash will actually be received.

Positive cash flow is absolutely crucial to the success of a business. Failure to have enough cash to meet the demands of creditors (those to whom the business owes money), will result in business being forced into liquidation.

Below is an example of a cash budget.

	£ Month 1 (£)	£ Month 2 (£)	£ Month 3 (£)
Opening balance	4,000	4,000	(2,500)
Cash in			
Sales cash	3,500	2,000	1,000
Sales credit	2,500	3,000	1,000
Loan			10,000
Total cash in	6,000	5,000	12,000
Total cash flow	10,000	9,000	9,500
Cash out			
Purchases cash	1,200	1,200	1,200
Purchases credit	1,300	1,300	1,300
Wages	2,000	2,500	3,000
Rent	1,000	1,000	1,000
Utility bills	500	500	500
Purchase of new machinery		5,000	
Total cash out	6,000	11,500	7,000
Closing balance	4,000	(2,500)	2,500

This is the cash at the start of the month.

List of actual money received.

Opening balance plus all cash in.

Real flow of money out of the business.

This is the total cash at the end of the month. Total cash flow less total cash out.

The closing balance for one month becomes the opening balance of the next.

TOP TIP

- 'Balance' means total.
- Brackets tend to show a negative figure.

A positive closing balance is known as a **surplus** and a negative closing balance is a **deficit**.

At Higher you will need to be able to interpret and offer solutions to potential cash-flow problems.

The table below explores the possible problems and solutions to the cash budget shown on page 63.

Problem	Possible solutions
Sales are falling while purchases are constant. *(Credit sales and credit purchases are transactions made in a previous month and only now is cash being received or paid.)*	• Reduce purchases (raw materials) to reflect falling sales. • Find a cheaper supplier of raw materials. • Encourage debtors, those who have bought sales on credit, to pay quicker by offering cash discounts. • Take advantage of the full credit period to delay paying for purchases. • Encourage sales by advertising.
Deficit cash balance in month 2	• Arrange the loan a month earlier. • Rent or lease new machinery rather than buy it.
Rising wage bill at the time of falling sales	• Reduce working hours. • Ban overtime payments. • Change payment system to be based on sales. • Terminate employment contracts, e.g. temporary staff. • Move production to another country with cheaper costs.

TOP TIP

A common mistake is that the **closing balance** is the same as profit. It is not and these terms must not be confused. If you sold a snowboard to a friend for £300, which had cost you £200 to buy, your cash inflow is £300 but your profit is only £100. Get it?

TOP TIP

Note that although the term **credit** is used for sales and purchases, this is the actual receipt and payment of cash albeit from transactions from an earlier period.

Quick Fire Questions

1.	Explain why positive cash flow is so important.
2.	What does the term 'balance' mean?
3.	What is the difference between a 'surplus' and a 'deficit' in a cash budget?
4.	Suggest one way of solving a negative cash flow in a business.
5.	What is the difference between cash flow and profit?
6.	Give examples of expenses in running a business.

Sample Examination Questions

1. Describe the role of the finance department in meeting the expectations of HM Revenue and Customs.
   2 marks

2. Describe reasons for cash-flow problems that can affect an organisation.
   5 marks

3. Describe the actions that could be taken to overcome cash-flow problems.
   5 marks

4. Describe reasons why an organisation would use cash budgets.
   5 marks

Financial statements

Two of the most important financial statement for any organisation are the **trading, profit and loss account** and the **balance sheet.** Collectively they are known as the **financial statements.**

For organisations in the private sector the main objective of most is profit maximisation. Profit can be defined as the difference between the money received from the sales and the costs of selling it.

The trading accounts shows the **gross profit** – the profit margin between sales and the costs of sales. The profit and loss shows the **net** profit – gross profit less any regular expenses involved in running a business.

Trading profit and loss accounts for Any Plc for the year ended 31 December, Year 1

		£	£	
	Sales		100,000	
	Opening stock	10,000		
(+)	Purchases	40,000		
		50,000		Trading
(−)	Closing stock	20,000		a/c
−	Cost of sales		30,000	
=	Gross profit		70,000	
	Wages	20,000		
	Bank loan interest	2,000		
	Utilities (electricity, gas, telephone)	5,000		Profit and
	Advertising	3,000		loss a/c
−	Expenses		30,000	
=	Net profit		£40,000	

Where expenses are larger than the gross profit a **net loss** is recorded.

Unit 2: Management of People and Finance

The balance sheet is a 'snap shot' of the business at a point in time.

Balance Sheet for Any Plc as at 31 December, Year 1

		£	£	
	FIXED ASSETS			
	Premises		*100,000*	
(+)	*Machinery*		*30,000*	
(+)	*Vehicles*		*20,000*	
			150,000	
	CURRENT ASSETS			
	Closing stock	*20,000*		
(+)	*Debtors*	*30,000*		Net
(+)	*Bank*	*15,000*		worth
(+)	*Cash*	*5,000*		section
		70,000		
	CURRENT LIABILITIES			
(−)	*Creditors*	*20,000*		
+	**Working capital**		**50,000**	
=	**Net worth**		**£200,000**	
	Financed by			
	Share capital		*100,000*	
(+)	*Net profits*		*40,000*	
			140,000	Financed
(−)	*Share dividends*		*30,000*	by
			110,000	section
(+)	*Mortgage and loans*		*90,000*	
			£200,000	

RULES OF DEBIT AND CREDIT

	INCREASE			DECREASE	
ASSET		DEBIT	ASSET		CREDIT
EXPENSE		DEBIT	EXPENSE		CREDIT
LIABILITY		CREDIT	LIABILITY		DEBIT
INCOME		CREDIT	INCOME		DEBIT
CAPITAL		CREDIT	CAPITAL		DEBIT

Glossary of terms

- **Fixed assets:** The items owned by the organisations that are intended to last for more than one year.
- **Current assets:** The items owned by the business that will constantly change over the year. These include **debtors**, who are customers who owe the business money – normally from buying on credit.
- **Current liabilities:** The items owed by the business. These will regularly change in value. These include **creditors**, who are suppliers who the business owes money to – usually from the purchasing of stock on credit.
- **Share capital:** The income received from shares bought by the shareholders.
- **Net profit:** The return for running a business and is brought forward from the trading, profit and loss account. Remember: it can also be a net loss.
- **Dividend:** The share of the net profit, which will go to the shareholders as a reward for investing in the business.
- **Mortgages and loans:** These are referred to as 'long-term liabilities' and help to finance the business. They are debts the business will need to pay back, but over a long period of time.

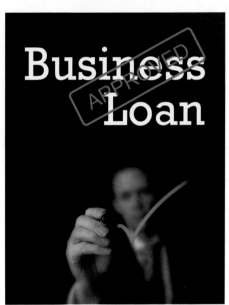

Quick Fire Questions

1. Name the statements that are referred to as the financial statements.
2. How is gross profit calculated?
3. How is net profit calculated?
4. Give an example of two common business expenses.
5. Giving examples, suggest the difference between fixed and current assets.

Sample Examination Question

Describe financial information that potential shareholders could use to decide whether or not to invest in a company.

6 marks

Ratio analysis

Ratios are a technique used to compare one figure with another. They are applied when comparisons are being made:

- between similar businesses
- against the industrial average
- within the same business, but between different years.

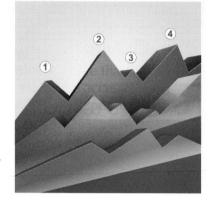

Different ratios can be used to measure different aspects of the business and fall into three general categories.

1. **Profitability ratios:** measuring the value of profit.
2. **Liquidity ratios:** showing the organisations' ability to meet its short-term debts.
3. **Efficiency ratios:** indicating how efficient the business has been in using its resources.

Profitability ratios

Profitability ratios are expressed as a **percentage**. A rising percentage or a bigger percentage than a rival is **good**.

Ratio	Formula	Interpretation	Reasons for improvements
Gross profit ratio	$\dfrac{gross\ profit}{sales} \times 100\%$ This ratio shows the amount of profit the business makes simply from buying and selling.	• A rise in this percentage would be indicating that the business is making more profit in relation to cost of sales. • A decrease would indicate the opposite.	• higher selling price. • lower cost of sales because of cheaper suppliers • lower cost of sales through better stock management, e.g. lower stock levels or less waste and/or theft
Net profit ratio	$\dfrac{net\ profit}{sales} \times 100\%$ This ratio shows the amount of profit the business earns after paying expenses.	• An increase in this percentage would show more profit in relation to all expenses. • A fall would suggest problems with expenses.	• an increase in the gross profit percentage • a fall in expenses in relation to the amount of sales*

*Sometimes expenses have to rise to increase sales, e.g. paying for more advertising. A positive net profit would indicate that sales have risen more than expenses.

Ratio	Formula	Interpretation	Reasons for improvements
Return on capital employed (ROCE)	$\dfrac{net\ profit}{capital\ employed} \times 100\%$ This ratio shows the maximum percentage return the shareholders could gain from their investment.	• An increase would suggest the business has done well making a healthy profit. • A fall in the percentage would suggest problems to do with falling sales or rising expenses.	• increase sales revenue without increasing the cost of sales by the same percentage • reducing expenses in relation to sales

Liquidity ratios

Liquidity ratios show the ability of a business to meet short-term debts. They are normally shown as a **ratio**. There are generally recognised ideal ratios, reducing the need for comparisons.

Ratio	Formula	Interpretation	Reasons for improvement
Current ratio	$\dfrac{current\ assets}{current\ liabilities} : 1$ This ratio shows the ability of the business to pay short-term debts. The ideal ratio is 2:1.	• A figure close to the ideal would suggest the business could meet its immediate debts should it have to. • It might seem strange that a business should not strive to have a much higher number of current assets to current liabilities, but too many current assets would show poor use of these reserves, e.g. large amounts of cash should be invested, 'employed', buying more fixed assets (such as machinery).	• a change in the number of current assets to current liabilities to reflect the ideal ratio of 2:1 • to reduce stock levels the business could adopt just-in-time (JIT) • be careful not to suggest changes that would have no impact, e. g. encouraging debtors to pay would certainly reduce the debtors figure, but would simply increase the amount in the bank resulting in no overall change

Ratio	Formula	Interpretation	Reasons for improvement
Acid test ratio	$\dfrac{current\ assets - stock}{current\ liabilities} : 1$ This ratio shows the ability of the business to pay short-term debts once stock is removed. The ideal ratio is 1:1.	• The stock figure is removed because stock is the most difficult to turn into cash. • A figure close to the ideal would suggest the business is being cautious.	• see current ratio reasons, with the obvious exception of stock in any analysis

TOP TIP

When carrying out ratio analysis, try to use more than one ratio.

Efficiency ratios

Efficiency ratios are expressed as a **number of times**, with the greater number normally regarded as better.

Ratio	Formula	Interpretation	Reasons for increase
Rate of stock turnover	$\dfrac{cost\ of\ sales}{average\ stock} = $ 'times' Average stock = (closing stock + opening stock) ÷ 2 This ratio shows the number of times that the entire stock is sold out during the year.	• A rising rate of stock turnover means that the stock is being sold more quickly, which generally would be regarded as a good thing by most businesses. • This figure should however be compared with profitability ratios, to ensure that the stock is not being given away at the expense of profit.	• increase in the cost of goods sold because of a rise in the cost of purchases • change in stock management resulting in cheaper stock or less stock being held e.g. move to JIT

Limitations of financial analysis

- The figures are based on historic data, and while past performance is a good indicator of future performance it is only a guide.
- Making comparisons between different organisations can be difficult because there are often many differences, e.g. size.
- External factors (PESTEC) are not taken into account.
- No consideration is taken of the stage in the product life cycle that the product being sold is at.
- Only financial information is considered, and so human resources are not factored in. For example, the recent retirement of an effective Chief Executive Officer (CEO) would be ignored.

Quick Fire Questions

1. The gross profit percentage for a business is 35% while the industrial average is 40%. Is this good or bad? Explain your answer.

2. How could the gross profit ratio be improved?

3. Does the gross profit ratio show the gross profit? If not where will you find the gross profit figure?

4. Suggest a reason for an improvement in the net profit ratio.

Sample Examination Questions

1. Describe the limitations of ration analysis.   **5 marks**

2. Describe three accounting ratios and justify their use (a different justification must be used each time).   **6 marks**

Sources of finance

Source of finance	Advantages	Disadvantages
Selling of shares This is only available to **limited** companies through selling equity (ownership) on the stock market. The company's memorandum of association and articles of association will set the number of shares that can be issued.	• Large sums of money can be generated. This is evident when the government has floated former public sector businesses, such as the Post Office moving them into the private sector. • The shares do not need to be paid back unlike a loan. • This is an attractive form of investment as it has limited liability.	• Equity or ownership is shared meaning more people are involved in decision-making. • Selling shares makes the organisation vulnerable to a takeover. • Dividends have to be shared amongst a larger group of investors.
Retained profits Once a business has been trading for some time it is likely to have built up reserves of profit which will allow it to reinvest in itself.	• No interest is chargeable. • There is no increase in ownership.	• Money cannot be used for something else. • Stakeholders can be unhappy because they might prefer the funds to be used for them, e.g. dividends for shareholders or increases wages for employees.
Government grants Businesses can qualify for Government/EU grants if they meet certain criteria, e.g. creating employment or becoming more environmentally friendly.	• Grants do not incur interest. • Grants do not have to be paid back.	• Grants are often very difficult and time-consuming to obtain. • Certain criteria need to be met or the grant can be withheld or withdrawn.
Venture capitalist **(business angels)** Other organisations or wealthy individuals invest in a business for a return on their investment.	• Finance can sometimes be available from Venture Capitalist when other lenders consider it too risky. • Sometimes the money comes with expertise and advice.	• A return must be made to the investor. • Often there are stipulations with the investment that will limit the freedom of the Board of Directors.

Source of finance	Advantages	Disadvantages
Leasing or hire purchase Rather than purchase a fixed asset, the business will rent it. With hire purchase, the asset belongs to the business on the final payment.	• There is no initial large investment. • As long as the product is rented any faults, breakdowns or maintenance will be fixed by the organisation that is renting out the item. • It gives the business time to see if it really needs the asset. • Updated models might become available.	• Costs could be higher in the long-term. • If payments are not maintained the asset will be repossessed.
Mortgage This is a loan secured on a fixed asset, normally property.	• This can secure a large amount of funds, which the lender is happier to lend because of the security. • Long period for repayment.	• If payments are not made, then the fixed asset will be sold to recover the debt. • Interest rates are likely to change over time, going up as well as down. • Often larger deposits are required by the borrower to secure the best interest rates.
Bank loan A negotiated loan from a bank paid over a period of time with interest.	• Set payments support effective budgeting.	• Interest is added to the sum borrowed.

Source of finance	Advantages	Disadvantages
Bank overdraft This is where more money is removed from the bank than is available. 	• It is often the only form of finance available. • It is often a quick way to obtain funds for a short period of time. • Interest is only charged on the amount outstanding, so early payments will reduce costs.	• There is a higher interest rate than a normal bank loan. • It can reduce the chances of other finance from the bank.
Trade credit In business, it is common practice to purchase items on credit and pay for them later.	• This allows a period where costs are not charged, helping cash flow.	• The business will not be able to take advantage of cash discount, which is a saving for prompt payment. • The amount must still be paid.
Debt factoring Debts are sold to a third party at a discount or subject to an administration fee.	• Funds are available sooner. • Transfers any risk of the debtor defaulting to the third party.	• Less money is received from the debt.

Quick Fire Questions

1. Suggest a benefit of selling shares.
2. What is the advantage of a grant over a loan?
3. Can you suggest an advantage over leasing a fixed asset rather than buying it?
4. Describe debt factoring.

Sample Examination Question

Describe and justify three sources of finance.

6 marks

Technology in finance

All large organisations will use software applications to record and process their financial transactions. These may be developed in-house by the IT department, or purchased from software developers who specialise in accounting packages such as Sage. In most cases, organisations will purchase software and then adapt it to their own particular requirements.

There has been an increase in the use of **cloud accounting** where businesses do not physically possess the software in their premises but simply access it on a rental basis from a remote site. This reduces short-term costs with no need for a dedicated server, and will ensure that accounting data is backed up. There are, however, concerns about the security of data held via a 'cloud'.

Accounting packages will be used to calculate payroll, track credit transactions and to produce cash budgets, financial statements and ratio analysis. One of the benefits of dedicated software is that a suite of specialised reports can be embedded within the system. These reports will quickly and accurately produce reports relevant to the business and aid in quick business decision-making. These systems can also link into external bodies, such as HMRC, to allow electronic submission of forms, such as VAT returns. This process will remove human error from the submission process, as it is an automatic submission from the system.

Most software packages have the added advantage that graphs can be produced that will highlight trends and variances.

Technology is never without costs. The price of software, hardware, technical support, and the increasing need for firewall security that will protect the organisations data, all adds up in cost.

TOP TIP

Higher Business Management is concerned with large organisations, so avoid IT solutions used by small businesses such as Microsoft Excel.

Quick Fire Questions

1. Why would large organisations use software applications?
2. Suggest three uses of accounting packages.
3. Describe a benefit of dedicated software.
4. What is the benefit of showing data in a graph?
5. Describe costs associated with technology.

Customers

Every business and organisation needs to know who their customers are and what their needs are. Customers are made up of different groups or segments, with their own particular characteristics and behaviour patterns. The table below shows some possible customer categories.

Category	Description
Age	Customers are often grouped according to age: teenagers have different wants and needs compared with 45–55 year olds. Customers aged 70+ have different needs and wants compared with both of these groups.
Gender	Males and females can have different tastes and spending patterns. This is not being stereotypical – merely stating the obvious.
Income	Customers with high disposable incomes have more to spend on luxury goods and services including holidays, cars and other leisure activities. Those on low incomes will spend more on basics such as food and clothing.
Social class	The jobs that people do are often categorised into different 'social classes'. People in any one particular class may have similar characteristics regarding how they spend their income.
Cultural/religious	Different faith groups may have an impact on spending patterns as well as cultural background, e.g. not eating certain foods.
Geographical location	Where customers live can have an impact on their spending, e.g. in the north of Scotland more is spent on travel than in a city.
Education	Sometimes the level of education attained can influence spending patterns, e.g. customers with a university degree may spend more on travel to different countries.
Family lifestyle	Families are made up of different sizes and patterns, e.g. living with parents is more common until our mid-20s than ever before. This changes how households spend their income.

Consumer behaviour

It is generally accepted that consumers will behave according to the broad categories in the table, so businesses find it easier to target customers for marketing purposes. Consumers want to feel satisfied with their purchases and feel that they have obtained good-quality products at a good price. Increasingly, they are also looking for good customer service and after-sales care.

Consumer behaviour will be affected by other factors too, such as personality, time of year, personal circumstances, family events, and economic factors such as recession and unemployment. Other consumer behaviour is based on routine purchases, for example, bread every day, cat food every week. Often consumers purchase on impulse – they see something they like and buy it without previously planning the purchase. Marketing campaigns and promotional offers also affect consumers.

Product-led and market-led business

- A **product-led business** will concentrate on their product without extensive market research or feedback. They are confident that their product is good quality and will sell, and there is usually no real competition in the market.

- A **market-led business** will concentrate on market research and will update and improve their product based on customers' needs and wants. They are constantly updating to make sure they can stay ahead of the competition and attract customers to their own products.

Quick Fire Questions

1. Describe two customer segments.
2. What factors influence consumer behaviour?

Sample Examination Question
Distinguish between product-led and market-led organisations.
2 marks

Market research 1

Market research involves gathering information about customers and markets. Market research is essential to the competitiveness of any business and to ensure that they improve their overall effectiveness. Market research is carefully planned and conducted regularly and the results of the research are analysed in order to aid decision-making.

Market research and improving effectiveness

Market research will usually involve gathering the following information.

- Who are the customers or potential new customers?
- What is their age group/income/location?
- What are their main preferences?
- What price are they willing to pay?
- Who are the competitors?
- What prices are they charging?
- What are the main features of their products and services?

Once this information has been gathered, businesses can use this information in the following ways.
- asking customers their opinions and altering the prices of their products
- asking customers to test out their products and changing the product in some way
- altering the place where the product is sold so that customers have easy access
- launching new advertising campaigns and using new advertising techniques
- offering new incentives and promotions to buy the product, for example, competitions, celebrity endorsement
- targeting brand new markets
- launching a new product in the correct way in order to avoid mistakes.

The main reasons for carrying out market research are to allow the business to increase market share, improve sales and profitability, and to make sure that customers get what they want. Businesses also want to improve their overall image and reputation and encourage customers to return in the future, ensuring customer loyalty. Returning customers will put the business ahead of the competition.

Sampling

In order to carry out field research, a business has to decide on what type of sampling they wish to carry out. Sampling involves selecting a group of consumers to ask questions – but the group must be chosen in some way.

It is impossible to ask questions of the whole population. The type of sampling carried out will depend on different factors:
- the type of product/service
- the location of the business

- what stage the product is at in terms of life cycle
- what other market research information already exists
- resources and budget available to the business.

Random sampling	This involves selecting groups of consumers at random, e.g. from the electoral register. Anyone can be chosen. This takes time to carry out, but is usually a good representation of the population as a whole.
Quota sampling	This involves selecting groups of the population that meet certain criteria or market segments, e.g. the sample may include 500 men and 500 women. This still gives a cross section of the population but is not completely random.
Systematic sampling	This involves selecting a section of the population at random and then deciding on the number to be sampled, e.g. choose a starting point and then deciding that every twentieth person will be sampled.
Convenience sampling	This involves taking responses from anyone who is willing to take part in the survey, however it can be biased if the same people volunteer over-and-over again.

Justifying the use of sampling methods

Market researchers have to make sure that they use a range of sampling methods in order to protect against issues that can arise:

- bias on the part of the interviewer
- unreliable or inaccurate responses from the interviewee
- errors in analysing the data
- faulty questionnaires
- lack of time available to gather the information.

The wider range of sampling carried out, the more reliable the information will be in terms of target market. Also, interviewers must be trained to avoid bias, but also to make sure they get the best responses from the public so that the data is as accurate as possible.

Quick Fire Questions

Sample Examination Question

Distinguish between quota sampling and random sampling.

3 marks

1. Outline three pieces of information that may be gathered during market research and suggest ways in which these pieces of information may be used by a business to improve effectiveness.

2. Outline two drawbacks from sampling.

3. Outline three methods of sampling.

4. What factors determine which method of sampling to be used.

Market research 2

Field research

Field research involves going out into the market place to gather first-hand information. This is called primary information. There are different methods of gathering this first-hand information.

Personal interview, questionnaire, survey	This can be done in different ways, e.g. face-to-face on the street, telephone survey, written questionnaire.
Technology survey	New technology allows customers to give personal feedback on websites or using mobile phones, e.g. online feedback forms or feedback after telephone calls.
Consumer panel or focus group	This is when a group of customers is brought together to discuss a product or service. Their individual responses and opinions are recorded and passed onto the business in order to make decisions.
Hall test	This involves giving a free sample or trial of a product to a group of customers and they are asked to give their opinion once they have tried it out.
Observation	A lot of information can be gathered by observing customers. Observations could take place in a shop, or in the high street. Behaviours can then be analysed.

> **TOP TIP**
> Field research is primary information. It is collected first-hand by the business for their own purposes.

Analysis of field research

Advantages	Disadvantages
The information gathered is relevant and includes personal opinions, which can be difficult to predict otherwise.	In order to obtain meaningful results, large numbers have to be interviewed.
The information is accurate and reliable, as the business knows how and when it was gathered.	It is very time-consuming to collect, as it can involve lengthy questionnaires and responses.
The information can be kept private from competitors, therefore businesses can improve their overall effectiveness in the market.	It is very expensive to carry out as researchers and analysts have to be employed to summarise what the data collected actually means.

Desk research

Desk research involves finding out information from existing sources. This is called **secondary information**. It involves using information that has already been gathered. There are different methods of gathering second-hand information.

Government data or statistics	The government publishes information from a variety of sources, e.g. the Census or Family Expenditure Survey.
Printed media, e.g. books, journals, newspapers	These contain information from a variety of sources about consumer behaviour and spending patterns.
Online research	There is a vast amount of data available from business websites, which can be used for market research purposes.

TOP TIP

There is a huge amount of information available on the Internet for businesses to access secondhand. However it is available to all businesses and may not always be relevant.

Analysis of desk research

Advantages	Disadvantages
The information is relatively cheap to obtain or may even be free.	The information may not be relevant to your business.
The information is usually easy to obtain and there is usually a large volume of information available.	The information may not always be accurate or up-to-date or totally reliable.
It is useful for analysing past trends in the market and therefore predicting future trends.	The information is freely available to competitors so it is not always helpful in gaining a competitive edge.

Quick Fire Questions

1. Outline two methods of field research.
2. Outline two disadvantages and two benefits of field research.
3. Outline two methods of desk research.
4. Give two disadvantages and two benefits of desk research.

Sample Examination Questions

1. Describe four methods of field research.
   7 marks

2. Describe and justify three market research techniques that an organisation could use to assess customer satisfaction. (A different justification should be used each time.)
   6 marks

The marketing mix: product

The marketing mix is often referred to as **the 4Ps**: product, price, place and promotion. Each of the 4Ps is unique in its own way, but the combination of the 4Ps allows a business to develop a marketing strategy that works and that enables products and services to be sold, and therefore profits made. The **extended marketing mix** includes three more Ps – people, process and physical evidence. These have been added because i) marketing is more customer-focused now than ever before, and ii) to take into account that more services are provided than ever before. There is more information about the extended marketing mix on pages 96–99.

> **TOP TIP**
>
> The extended marketing mix includes the 7 Ps: product, price, place, promotion, people, process and physical evidence.

Product

This is the product or service that is being sold by the business. The product will have been developed by the business and marketed to customers.

The product life cycle

Most products go through a recognised cycle during their life. The product life can be short or long, but the stages are the same. The stages of the product life cycle are shown below.

Development	Research and development of the product involves developing a prototype and test marketing in order to get feedback from customers.
Introduction	The product is introduced or launched onto the market.
Growth	Once customers know about the product, sales begin to grow.
Maturity	Everyone who wants the product has already purchased it and sales level out. At this stage, the business may want to introduce extension strategies in order to prolong the life of the product.
Saturation	At the very end of the maturity stage, the product is saturated and no further growth is possible.
Decline	Sales of the product start to fall because there are no new customers.

The product life cycle is shown on the graph below.

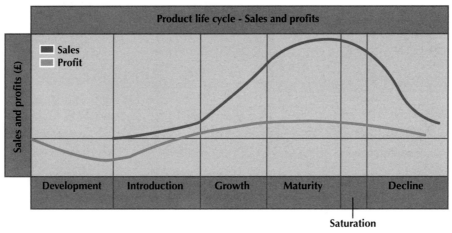

Sales and profits in the product life cycle

During the research and introduction stages of the product, sales and profits are low. There are costs associated with developing and launching the product onto the market. However, as sales begin to rise, profits also begin to rise. At the maturity stage, sales and profits will be at their highest. In order to ensure continued sales and profits, the business has to consider extension strategies. Eventually, as saturation and decline sets in, sales and profits begin to fall until the product is removed from the market.

Extension strategies

In order to revive or prolong the life cycle of a product, the business may wish to use extension strategies. These usually involve changing the 7 Ps in some ways as explained below.

Product	Altering the product in some way, e.g. new packaging, new taste, new flavour, new size or weight of the product. Usually a fairly subtle change so that customers still want the updated version. Or alternatively, finding new markets or uses for existing products.
Price	Altering the price – usually a decrease in the price, but this can be for a limited period to boost demand.
Place	Altering the places where the product can be sold, e.g. introducing online ordering or home delivery or extending into more retailers.
Promotion	Changing the advertising and promotion campaigns to make more customers aware of the product, e.g. new BOGOF offers or celebrity endorsement.
People	For example, training the people who have provided the service to ensure that the customers are happy.
Process	Updating and examining the processes involved in delivery of the service, e.g. having to wait too long for service or attention.
Physical evidence	Ensuring that the physical evidence shows that the service that took place is positive rather than negative.

Extension strategies are shown on the graph below.

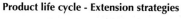

Product life cycle - Extension strategies

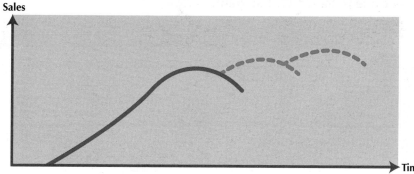

Product line portfolios

Many businesses have more than just one product to sell to customers. They have a range of product lines, known as a **product portfolio**. For example, Ford, Vauxhall and Mazda have one than one car in their ranges, and Cadbury's, Nestle and Kellogs all have more than one food product in their ranges to sell to customers too.

Businesses with a range of products – a product portfolio – will expect to have these products at different stages of the product life cycle. This can mean that as some products are going into decline, other products are being introduced onto the market. Overall, this has the effect of keeping sales and profits at an even level.

The benefits of product line portfolios are weighed up in the table below.

TOP TIP

Many large businesses in the food industry are good examples of product line portfolios, for example Heinz, Kellogs, Baxters.

Advantages	Disadvantages
Customers will already know the existing product lines, and therefore new ones can be introduced quickly.	If there is a problem with one product it can affect the reputation of all the products in the line.
Risk of failure is spread across a range of products.	The business may have to invest heavily in machinery and equipment to make a range of different product lines.
Market share can be increased as different products will appeal to different market segments.	The business will continually have to train staff to produce new products in the product line.

Diversified product portfolios

Businesses with a diversified product portfolio have a range of products that are aimed at different market segments. The Virgin Group is a good example, as it provides a range of media services as well as transport and financial products.

The aim of the business is to increase sales and profits over a wide range of products, but also to spread the risks if any one particular product fails. Unilever is another example of a business with a very wide diversification of products. Diversification can be horizontal (when the new products are all at the same stage in the production process) or conglomerate (when the new products are at different stages in the production process).

As you can see from the picture, Unilever provides food products (for example, Cornetto ice-creams) and cleaning products (for example, Surf washing powder).

Analysis of diversified product portfolios

Advantages	Disadvantages
• Selling a variety of products can increase the profits. • It is easier to increase brand awareness. • New products can be launched easily as they will be recognised. • A range of products spreads the risk of failure. • Changes in demand or seasonal demand are easier to cope with. • A wider market can be targeted with different products.	• Advertising costs can be high, as the business has to make sure that all their products are advertised. • It can be expensive to continually research and develop new products to keep a large portfolio. • One product may cause a problem that can affect the whole portfolio.

Quick Fire Questions

1. Describe the stages of the product life cycle.
2. Describe two product extension strategies.
3. Explain the term product line portfolio.
4. Give two disadvantages and two benefits of a diversified product portfolio.
5. Give two examples of businesses that offer a diversified product portfolio.

Sample Examination Questions

1. Describe the four main stages of the product life cycle.

    4 marks

2. Describe the effect of each stage on profits.

    4 marks

3. Explain how various methods of extending a product's life cycle can increase sales.

    6 marks

The marketing mix: price

The price of any product is extremely important and extremely sensitive to the demands of the market. There are a number of factors that need to be considered when setting prices for a product.

- What did it cost to make?
- What price are competitors charging?
- Is the product sensitive to very small changes in price?

Businesses usually adopt a pricing strategy based on the above factors. The most common pricing strategies are as follows:

- **High price:** Setting a higher price for the product than competitors, as the business is confident that consumers will pay it.
- **Low price:** Setting a lower price for the product than competitors, as the business wants to try and undercut the competition.
- **Cost plus pricing:** This is based on the cost of the product to produce. The manufacturer then decides on how much they want to make in terms of profit and add this on – usually as a percentage of the cost.
- **Penetration pricing:** This is setting a price low to begin with in order to penetrate the market. Once the product is established, the price will increase.
- **Price skimming:** This is charging a high price for a product that is new and perhaps a bit different. Customers are happy to pay the high price, as they associate the product with prestige or status.
- **Destroyer pricing:** This is setting a low price, with the aim of destroying the competition. Once the competition has been destroyed, the business can raise the price again, as there will be no other business supplying the product.
- **Psychological pricing:** Setting a price to elicit an emotional response in the consumer, for example, setting prices at £4.95 or £2.98 (consumers think they are much lower prices than they actually are).

Use of technology in pricing

Consumers now have access to a wide range of information about prices that enables them to make more informed purchasing decisions. For example, business websites usually include prices of products as well as discounts, offers and promotions available. Consumers can find out this information online before they go shopping.

Price comparision websites such as www.moneysupermarket.com allow consumers to compare prices for a range of products and services to make sure they get the best deal. Price comparison websites are extremely useful for businesses because they are placed in the running for customers to choose from. However, these websites can be complicated and they do not always compare like with like. Regardless, many large companies are now linked to these websites.

> **TOP TIP**
>
> Pricing strategies and decisions are now crucial to the success of a business because competition is so fierce, and customers are much more knowledgeable about the competition.

Quick Fire Questions

1. Outline two factors to be taken into account when setting prices.
2. Compare high and low pricing strategies.
3. Explain how cost plus pricing works.
4. What is psychological pricing?
5. How do customers use price comparison websites?

Sample Examination Questions

1. Describe two pricing tactics that an organisation could use when selling an exclusive product.   **4 marks**

2. Describe three pricing tactics that could be used when an organisation attempts to break into a new market.   **6 marks**

The marketing mix: place

The place element of the marketing mix has changed considerably in the last ten years. Place refers to how the product gets to the consumer and where it is sold.

Products get to consumers in a variety of different ways – often referred to as channels of distribution. This means how the product is transported and distributed to the consumer. There are four main channels.

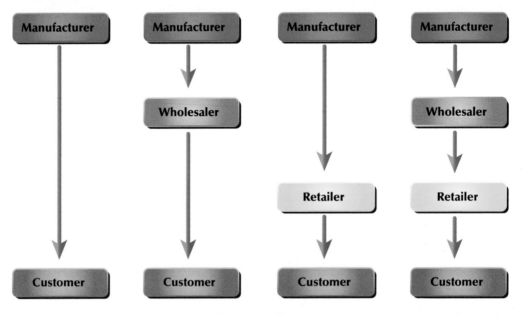

The table below weighs up the benefits of using different types of distribution channels.

Distribution channel	Advantages	Disadvantages
Wholesalers	For the consumer or small business outlet – the bulk is broken down so they can buy in small amounts For the small business – the wholesaler may provide some discounts for buying in bulk	For the consumer – increased prices compared to direct sales For the manufacturer – the wholesaler needs to be reliable, and promote and sell the product in the way they want
Retailers	For the consumer – a local place to buy products and to obtain advice and after-sales service; they can also get finance and delivery for large items For the manufacturer – the retailer provides information and advice, promotion and advertising for the products they wish to get to the consumers; the choice of retailer may contribute to the success overall of the product	For the consumer – sometimes too much choice, or retailers deciding which products they wish to sell rather than what consumers really want For the manufacturer – they have to rely on the retailer promoting and selling the product in the way they want For the manufacturer – deciding on which type of retailer to choose to sell their products can be a problem (e.g. mainstream fashion, aspirational or luxury)

Distribution channel	Advantages	Disadvantages
Direct sales	For the consumer – direct selling usually means a more tailor-made product for their own requirements  For the manufacturer – they can maintain contact with their customers to ensure they provide what they want	For the consumer – there may not be a wide choice, therefore prices can be difficult to negotiate For the manufacturer – they need to employ additional staff to do the selling

The role of the wholesaler and retailer

The **wholesaler is** often referred to as the 'middleman'. They are the link between the manufacturer and the retailer. The manufacturer needs to get their goods out into the market for customers to buy them as soon as possible. Wholesalers offer this service to the manufacturer. They 'buy up' the finished products from the manufacturer and sell them onto the retailer. Wholesalers buy in bulk, as they have the space to store large quantities of products in the correct conditions. They then break down the 'bulk' and sell to retailers in smaller quantities for them to sell in their shops.

Wholesalers also buy from different manufacturers, so the retailer can have a choice of different products. The wholesaler often gives credit to the retailers to enable them to stock their shops with the range and variety of products that customers want.

The **retailer** is the last link in the chain of distribution. They provide the goods and services that customers want. They enable customers to buy in small quantities from locations that are suitable for them. They provide personal service and contact with the customers. They provide before- and after-sales service and advice. They also provide choice.

The retailer also feeds back to the wholesaler on market trends, consumer preferences and demand. The wholesaler can then adjust their stock requirements so that they are not left with unsold stocks in their warehouses.

Types of retailer

There are a wide variety of retailers in the UK today – both on the high street and online. Broadly speaking they come under the following headings.

- **Independent retailers:** These are usually small shops that sell a very limited range of goods, for example, corner grocery stores, hat shops, fishing supplies and bicycle shops. They are often operated as sole graders.
- **Multiple chain stores:** These are spread over the country and are the same wherever you find them, for example, Marks and Spencer, Top Shop, Office, Homebase, B&Q, Boots and Superdrug. They can sell a wide range of products or specialise in a smaller area. They usually have an online store that provides a delivery service to customers.
- **Supermarkets:** These offer food and non-food products and are well known throughout the country, for example, Tesco, ASDA, Morrisons and Sainsburys.
- **Department stores:** They are also found throughout the country, but there are fewer of them and they usually stock more specialised and up-market brands, for example, Debenhams, John Lewis and House of Fraser.
- **Franchises:** They are operated by individuals who have purchased the rights to trade under the 'brand name', for example, McDonalds, The Body Shop and Pizza Hut.
- **Mail order/catalogues:** Most catalogues now provide online shopping services, where customers can place orders for goods to be delivered straight to their homes. Some companies still send out copies of their catalogues for customers to place orders by mail.
- **TV shopping channels:** Many manufacturers offer their products for sale via TV shopping channels, for example QVC. The channel may specialise in one particular product, for example, jewellery or offer a wide variety of products.

Methods of distribution

Products have to be transported from the manufacturer to where they are going to be sold – be it wholesaler, retailer or direct sales. There are different methods to choose from depending on many factors:

- distance to travel
- volume of products to be transported
- environmental factors
- availability of infrastructure, for example, railway, motorway.

TOP TIP

Do not become confused between the terms channels of distribution and methods of distribution. Check that you know their meanings.

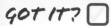
The table below shows the advantages and disadvantages of different distribution methods.

Method of distribution	Advantages	Disadvantages
Road network	• very quick to deliver in cities • cheaper than other methods • good road network in UK	• petrol • vehicles • insurance • pollution
Rail network	• quick service from city to city • good for large products and large volumes of deliveries	• train service • some areas of the country do not have a reliable rail service
Aeroplane	• quick to distribute products over a long distance • can be used for small quantities	• airline service • getting to airport • not suitable for large products
Sea	• can be useful for large quantities to be transported long distances if time is not an issue	• vessel • costs to getting to docks • some areas of the country are not close to docks • journey can take a long time

Quick Fire Questions

1. Describe two channels of distribution.
2. Outline two benefits of using wholesalers.
3. Outline two benefits of using retailers.
4. Name three methods of distribution of finished products.
5. Outline two disadvantages of transporting by sea.

Sample Examination Questions

1. Describe the reasons why some manufacturers sell their products to retailers rather than directly to customers.
   4 marks

2. Describe the advantages and disadvantages of methods of physical distribution that a producer could use to get their product to consumers.
   5 marks

3. Explain the advantages and disadvantages of using a wholesaler.
   5 marks

The marketing mix: promotion

Promotion is aimed at two distinct groups – those who will sell the product (retailers) and those who will buy the product (consumers).

Into the pipeline promotions

These are aimed at retailers who agree to sell the finished products from the manufacturer. There are a number of different promotions:

- **dealer promotions and loaders,** such as prizes given to the retailer that sells the most of the product, or extra products given for volume, for example one free box of sweets for every five boxes stocked
- **point of sale displays** including posters, stands, free samples
- **staff training** on the product features and advantages so that they can deal confidently with consumers who are purchasing
- **extended credit** given to enable retailers to purchase stock.

Out of the pipeline promotions

These are aimed at consumers in order to persuade them to buy products. There are a number of different promotions:

- discounts
- special offers – buy one get one free
- free samples or tasting
- price reductions, for example, 65p off for a limited period only
- loyalty cards
- celebrity endorsement
- vouchers or coupons
- free entry into competitions.

These promotions are effective in the short-term as they attract consumers' attention. There is a wide variety of choice for consumers, so the difference between purchasing one product and another may just be the fact that on the day there was a free sample given away, or a price reduction or entry into a competition.

TOP TIP

Promotions are very good for increasing sales in the short-term.

Public relations

The way that businesses and organisations are perceived by the public is often managed by proactive 'public relations' (PR). There may be a separate department or section in the business or organisation that deals specifically with PR. Indeed, many celebrities have their own PR assistant who deals exclusively with their public image.

PR involves providing information about products and services – and the business in general – that shows the business in a positive way. This can involve working closely with the marketing and advertising team; and may involve releasing press statements, gaining publicity for making charity donations, engaging celebrities for advertising or product endorsements and sponsoring events such as sports. Most importantly, it can involve damage limitation to the business reputation when things go wrong, such as industrial action, faulty products, accidents in the workplace or bad customer feedback. An effective PR team will anticipate problems before they develop into something that can seriously damage the business' reputation.

Advertising

Businesses advertise their products through a range of different media, but their choice will depend on whether they wish their advertising to be **above the line** or **below the line**.

Above the line

Above the line advertising targets a mass audience but the business does not really have much control over who actually sees the advert. Television, cinema and newspaper advertising are examples of above the line advertising. This type of advertising is expensive, but it can be less effective as it is difficult to appeal to such large audiences and have a message that appeals or is remembered by everyone.

Below the line

Below the line advertising is more targeted at a particular audience and is more effective as it is tailored to their needs. Examples are direct mail, direct selling, sponsorship and social media where the business has much more control over who sees the advert. The recent impact of social media on platforms such as Facebook and Twitter is huge, as companies can display advertisements on these sites, but individuals will also talk to one another about these companies and their products. Of course, the talk can be positive or negative.

Ethical marketing practices

The growth of media and personal electronic devices has led to an increase in the number of people who can be targeted directly for advertising. This can be through text messages, Facebook, Twitter, email, etc. However, not all individuals want or need this type of approach and this can be viewed as an invasion of privacy.

Advertising and promotion have become much more sophisticated because of multimedia approaches, so there is a growing need to make sure that adverts are honest, impartial and objective, and not just aiming to make profits at the expense of individuals. Ethical marketing avoids businesses making claims that products are going to change people's lives, and protects vulnerable groups such as elderly people or those on low incomes.

Advertising in the UK is regulated by the Advertising Standards Authority, which states that advertising must be legal, decent, honest and truthful. They have a code that businesses must adhere to and adverts can be withdrawn if they break this code.

TOP TIP

Remember that not all customers feel that advertising through text messages, Facebook and Twitter is positive. It can put off customers as well as attract them.

Quick Fire Questions

1. Distinguish between 'into the pipeline' and 'out of the pipeline' promotions.

2. Explain 'above the line' and 'below the line' advertising.

3. Explain the impact of social media advertising.

4. Explain what ethical marketing is.

5. What can customers do if they feel adverts are misleading?

Sample Examination Question

Organisations use various forms of advertising media to bring their products to the attention of consumers. Describe and justify different forms of advertising media.

6 marks

The extended marketing mix

The extended marketing mix

As mentioned at the beginning of this chapter, the marketing mix has now been extended to include the 7 Ps. The three additional Ps are people, process and physical evidence, and they are important in the delivery of services, rather than businesses that provide tangible products.

People

The 'people' part of the extended marketing mix includes employees, managers and customers.

Employees have to be trained appropriately to make sure they have the skills, knowledge and expertise to do their jobs properly and to a high standard. This also includes customer service training if employees are dealing directly with the public. Anyone who comes into contact with customers makes an important impression about the business overall – therefore it has to be positive and impressive. Customers have so much choice today that the employees need to make that vital first impression.

Employees also have to be continually developed in their role by continuous professional development, target setting and appraisal systems. Employees are one of the greatest assets that a business has, but they are also one of the most expensive. Therefore it is worthwhile investing in them.

Managers have to be highly trained in making decisions and using limited resources wisely. They will make decisions at a strategic and tactical level about the overall direction the business is heading. They must be given the right level of authority and responsibility to let the business be successful, but also challenged if this does not happen. Managers have to develop corporate culture and wellbeing so that employees feel valued and motivated at work.

Managers have to encourage enterprising skills and attitudes in their employees in order to stay competitive. They must be prepared to take risks with research, innovation, and new ideas. They need to ensure that market research and customer feedback is acted upon quickly and effectively.

Managers have to set targets for employees that are realistic and achievable. They should provide the appropriate balance of support and encouragement, as well as performance management for employees who are not delivering.

Customers have to be treated with respect and care. Customer service policies must be put into practice and customers must be informed regularly about services on offer. Customers must be offered before- and after-sales advice. Customer enquiries should be answered quickly and a variety of options offered. After-sales service in the form of follow-ups, guarantees and refunds are extremely important for customer loyalty and retention.

Many businesses and organisations undertake the 'Investors in People' award to demonstrate to their customers the standards of customer care they can expect.

Process

In order to deliver an efficient service there must be 'process' in place so that everyone knows what to do, when to do it and how to do it. For example, when you attend school you are marked present on a register in the classroom. This information is transferred to the school office. If you are absent, the school office contact your parents, and also contact pastoral care. This does not happen by accident. This is a planned process that takes place every day and everyone knows their role.

The process of giving a service is crucial to customer satisfaction. Customers are often in a hurry and do not have time to wait or be offered lengthy explanations or systems that are confusing or time-consuming.

The 'process' of delivering the service to customers has to be robustly tried and tested. If the service is sloppy, slow or inefficient, customers have a choice and will go elsewhere.

There are different processes depending on the services being provided. A small hairdresser will provide very personal contact with the customer as soon as they enter the salon. The customer will expect them to be on time and be offered refreshments if there is any delay. However, a large business providing home or car insurance will have a different process. This could be an application on a website followed-up with documents received through the post; or it could be an agent providing a home visit with a quote that is then followed-up with the correct documents. Either way, the process has to be accessible for the customer, easy to complete and achieved within an acceptable time period.

Customers are put off by lengthy conversations to call centres that involve being passed from one operator to another or pressing numerous buttons to navigate around the system.

Restaurants, bars and cafes involve different processes again. Customers expect food to be served appropriately and within an acceptable time period. Busy restaurants with lengthy waiting times and substandard goods or services will not be tolerated by customers who have a choice.

Physical evidence

The physical evidence relates to where the service is being delivered from. Customers cannot 'see' the service in advance so they need to have confidence that the service will be acceptable. The physical evidence they see takes many different forms.

- **Physical environment:** This can be the physical building as well as the image of employees. Buildings and reception areas should be bright and welcoming for customers. Any area of the business that customers see should provide confidence that the service will match up to the same standard. Reception areas should provide refreshments, toilets and waiting areas that are comfortable. Additional facilities could be magazines, WiFi access, toys for children, plasma screens with messages, advertising materials.

- **Business image:** This can also be the corporate image of the business, for example logos, signs, and other distinguishing features, such as specific colours, artefacts, displays and advertising materials. The ambience of the building is also very important. A business offering medical services would have a crisp clean ambience that demonstrated hygiene. Whereas a business offering entertainment should have a relaxed ambience with music playing and bright cheerful colours.

- **Employees:** They should portray the overall image of the business. This could be a uniform, for example, banks, travel agents and supermarkets usually have an employee uniform. Employees should have name badges and always use customers' names when talking to them personally.

- **Customer service:** There should be evidence of customer satisfaction, for example, testimonials, feedback forms, photographs etc. There should be a written policy of customer service as well as complaints procedures. Contact details as well as telephone numbers should be visible and easily accessible for customers.

- **Company details:** The company mission statement, vision and values should be clearly displayed as well as an organisation chart that shows employees, managers and contact details within the business. Details of awards or quality improvements should be visible to customers to give them confidence. Many of these features can also be displayed on business websites.

Quick Fire Questions

1. What are the three additional Ps of the extended marketing mix?

2. What role do employees play in the 'people' part of the extended marketing mix?

3. What physical features should customers experience in the 'physical evidence' part of the extended marketing mix?

Stock management

Management of stock is an important element of operations, as stocks of raw materials are needed in order to manufacturer the finished goods. There are different methods and systems of stock management.

Just-in-time (JIT) stock control

TOP TIP

JIT stock control is sometimes referred to as JIT production.

JIT stock control is a system where stocks are ordered to arrive just before they are needed. In other words, the business does not hold large amounts of stock in warehouses or store rooms. JIT system needs an excellent relationship with suppliers so that stocks arrive when they are needed, otherwise there is a danger that production will have to be stopped.

The table below weighs up the benefits of JIT stock control.

Advantages	Disadvantages
JIT avoids warehouse costs or stock room costs, and therefore production costs are lower.	Suppliers must be reliable for stocks to arrive on time.
JIT avoids deterioration of stock that has not been stored properly.	It can be difficult to respond quickly to changes in demand.
JIT avoids stocks going out-of-date or fashion too quickly.	Administration and ordering systems must be reliable.
JIT avoids theft or pilfering of stock therefore improving profit figures.	Delays in transport or adverse weather conditions can hold up deliveries.

Storage and warehousing of stocks

Unlike JIT, other systems of stock management involve holding stocks in the factory or warehouse. Stock levels are determined as set out in the table below.

Maximum stock level	This is the highest level of stock that the business will hold, in order to minimise costs and make the most efficient use of the space. The level depends on usage and delivery times.
Minimum stock level	This is the lowest level that stock should not fall below, in order to make sure that there are no shortages, and production does not have to be stopped. The level depends on usage.
Re-order level	This is the level at which more stock should be ordered, in order to make sure that stock does not drop below the minimum level.

| Re-order quantity | This is the amount of stock that is ordered, in order to bring the stock back up to the maximum level. |
| Lead time | This is the amount of time it takes between ordering new stock and the stock arriving in the business. |

Stock storage conditions are outlined below.

- The warehouse or stock room should be well-lit, dry and well ventilated.
- A system should be used for booking stock in and out of the warehouse.
- Stock should be used on a first in, first out basis.
- Accurate records should be kept of stock levels.
- Warehouses or stock rooms should be supervised and locked.
- Appropriate space should be given to stock items.
- All shelves and storage areas should be labelled for easy access.

Logistical management of stock

The process of stock management and control is highly sophisticated and controlled, and is often referred to as **logistics**. This starts at the supply chain and moves through to the consumer receiving the finished product. At each stage in this process, costs and profits are essential – therefore waste has to be avoided.

The benefits to a business overall of managing stock systems are enormous.

- Customers should always receive their orders on time.
- Stocks of raw materials should never run out.
- Administration costs should be controlled, as stock is ordered at regular intervals.
- There is less possibility of under- or over-stocking.
- Less storage space is needed for stock, therefore costs can be reduced.
- There will also be less wastage and theft of stock.

Quick Fire Questions

1. What is meant by JIT stock control?
2. Outline two disadvantages and two benefits of JIT stock control.
3. Explain the role of suppliers in a JIT stock control system.
4. Explain the terms maximum and minimum stock.
5. Describe the features of a suitable stock warehouse.

Sample Examination Questions

1. Explain the problems that can arise from 'under' and 'over' stocking.

   4 marks

2. Discuss the use of just-in-time production.

   6 marks

Production

Production of finished goods can be either labour intensive or capital intensive.

- In **labour intensive** production, people do most of the production, rather than machines. People use their skills and knowledge, although there may be some use of machinery.

- In **capital intensive** production, machines are mostly used – normally in factories with production lines and very large numbers of products produced.

Capital intensive production can be **mechanised** (using machines, but with people involved) or **automated** (systems where there are no humans involved in the production process at all and robots and machinery do all the work).

Type of production	Advantages	Disadvantages
Labour intensive	• Humans can use their skills and abilities and their initiative. • Humans are able to respond to changes quickly.	• Humans are expensive to pay and train. • Absenteeism can cost the business. • Humans can make errors and need rest breaks.
Capital intensive	• Machines can work 24 hours a day. • Machines can do boring repetitive jobs with a high degree of accuracy.	• Machines are expensive to install and maintain. • When machines break down production stops. • It is difficult to adapt machines quickly to changes in the product.

Methods of production

Production can be organised in three different ways: job production, batch production and flow production. The three methods are outlined below.

Job production

This is usually defined as one 'job' done at a time by an individual skilled worker. The job is often made to the specific requirements of the customer, which are agreed in advance. The job involves a high degree of skill on behalf of the employees and the job can take a long time to complete.

Advantages	Disadvantages
The product is made to the specific requirements of the customer.	Can take a long time to produce.
High prices can be charged for the skill and expertise involved.	Production costs are also high because there are no opportunities for economies of scale to be made.

Batch production

This is usually defined as groups of products that are made at the same time – in batches. Each product in the batch is the same, but there may be slight variations between batches. Batch production is commonly used in the food industry, but also for other products such as paint and wallpaper.

Advantages	Disadvantages
Production costs can be reduced because many products can be made at the same time.	Switching between batches can be time-consuming if changes to machinery need to be made.
There can still be some degree of tailoring the batches to the customer's requirements.	If there is a problem with one product in the batch, the whole batch may be affected.

Flow production

This is usually defined as very large numbers of products produced continuously on a production line. It is often referred to as 'mass production' or 'line production', as the goods are made on production lines. Flow production is common in the car industry, where cars are made in stages along the production line with the use of robots and machinery.

Advantages	Disadvantages
Very large numbers of products can be made quickly at the same time, thus lowering unit costs of production.	The product is exactly the same for each customer – there is no tailoring to their requirements.
The use of machinery allows the production process to be running constantly (often fully automated).	There are very little opportunities for employees to use their skills and initiative – many of the tasks involved are boring and repetitive.
Quality assurance can be built into each stage of the production process.	There are very high costs involved for machinery and production lines.

Quick Fire Questions

1. Distinguish between labour intensive and capital intensive production.

2. Distinguish between mechanisation and automation.

3. Give examples of job, batch and flow production.

4. Outline one advantage and one disadvantage of batch production.

5. Outline one advantage and one disadvantage of flow production.

Sample Examination Questions

1. Describe three different types of production that could be used by an organisation.

   3 marks

2. Explain the advantages and disadvantages of using job production.

   5 marks

Quality

Quality means different things to different people. A quality product involves the following:

- using high quality raw materials
- training employees regularly and to a high standard
- using up-to-date machinery and equipment
- appropriate packaging
- the product being delivered on time
- being produced to quality standards, such as the BSI Kitemark ™.

Quality circles

This involves groups of employees coming together with the management in order to discuss issues of quality. Employees are usually trained to identify, analyse and solve some of the problems in their work. They would then present solutions to management and, where possible, implement the solutions themselves. One of the aims is to give employees more responsibility and increased motivation.

Quality control

This involves checking products after they have been produced to make sure they meet the standards expected. If a product fails the quality check, it is discarded or recycled back into the production process. Quality control can be wasteful if it is only carried out at the end of the production process.

Quality assurance

This involves a planned and systematic approach to checking products at more regular intervals during the production process and trying to avoid problems happening in the first place. Quality assurance involves the whole production process, starting with good-quality raw materials. If quality assurance checks are carried out, employees are more confident that the completed product will be acceptable to customers.

Total quality management

This involves every employee in the organisation ensuring that quality is built in at each and every stage of the production process. It is an overall business philosophy designed to ensure customer satisfaction. It ensures that quality raw materials are purchased from reliable suppliers. Any errors or problems in the production process are eliminated and the failure rate of finished products is very low indeed.

All staff, including office staff, are involved in the quality process. Often organisations have quality awards for their high standards, such as: Investors in People, Charter Marks or the BSI Kitemark. Customers know, therefore, that the product is good quality.

TOP TIP

Make sure you understand the difference between quality control, quality assurance and total quality management.

Quality standards and symbols

In the UK there are recognised systems of quality standards, for example, the BSI (British Standards Institution) Kitemark scheme. British Standards cover a wide range of businesses and products. Another standard is ISO 9001, an international standard for quality management.

Benchmarking

Benchmarking is an approach to quality that involves the business applying a set of standards or benchmarks. The business has to make sure that it achieves these benchmarks in order to stay competitive. Benchmarking can be internal or external.

Internal benchmarking involves setting standards within the organisation that are then used to compare performance across different departments. External benchmarking involves setting standards within the industry for each business to measure themselves against.

Mystery shopping

The use of a mystery shopper has grown in recent years as an indicator of quality. This can be used to gauge the quality of a product or a service. Typically, a member of the public is trained to act as a 'normal' shopper, when in fact they are analysing and evaluating their shopping experience or the quality of the product. The employees of the business are unaware that this is taking place, so very important and accurate feedback can be received about the customer experience.

Analysis of quality management activities

Advantages	Disadvantages
• Feedback from customers, which will inform improvements to products and customers. • Customers will be more satisfied, therefore they will be willing to return and to pass on the good reputation of the business. • Employees will be more satisfied and more motivated in their jobs. • Good-quality products will reduce waste. • Profits can be increased.	• Higher costs of raw materials. • Staff training costs. • Costs of applying and maintaining quality awards and standards. • Employees can be reluctant to constantly strive for improvements if they feel under pressure.

Quick Fire Questions

1. Outline the meaning of the term quality.
2. Describe the following – quality control, quality circles.
3. How does total quality management ensure customer satisfaction?
4. Describe how benchmarking works.
5. What are the advantages of using a mystery shopper?

Sample Examination Question

Describe quality management systems that can be used within an organisation.

7 marks

Ethical issues

Businesses now operate in an environment that is extremely competitive but also demanding from the point of view of customers. Customers look for products that have been produced in an ethical way and do not damage the environment. There are also laws in place to protect the environment, which businesses must adhere to.

Ethical issues

One of the main ethical issues is the concept of fair trade. Businesses are encouraged to adopt fair trade principles and customers often support products that have been produced by fair trade companies or countries. In the UK, the Fairtrade Foundation says:

Fairtrade is about better prices, decent working conditions, local sustainability, and fair terms of trade for farmers and workers in the developing world.

Our vision is of a world in which justice and sustainable development are at the heart of trade structures and practices so that everyone, through their work, can maintain a decent and dignified livelihood and develop their full potential.

www.fairtrade.org.uk

Fairtrade products include a range of food products, for example bananas, coffee, tea, as well as flowers, cotton, etc. The Fairtrade foundation licences products as being fairtrade and allows them to display the logo.

Analysis of Fairtrade

Advantages	Disadvantages
Customers are happy to buy fair trade products so there will be increased customer loyalty.	Prices are higher both for the manufacturer who buys fair trade raw materials and the consumer who buys the final product.
Most businesses who are licensed for fair trade enjoy a good reputation and public image, and therefore employees are easier to recruit.	Many of the products have to be transported a long way across the world leading to issues of environmental pollution.

·Ethical operations

In addition to fair trade, there are other operational issues that businesses should avoid to be considered ethical. Ethical behaviour is any behaviour that is fair and just and does not have an adverse impact on people or countries. It is also behaviour that does not break the law. Some examples of that are ethical and therefore positive business practices are:

- not using child labour or 'sweat shops' to produce goods
- making sure that all employees are treated fairly and justly, for example, complying with the Equality Act 2010
- making sure that all Health and Safety laws and practices are taken into account, and not cutting corners in order to save money.

The benefits to business from engaging in ethical practices lie in the trust that both customers and employees have. Customers will consistently buy from the business, and employees will be loyal and motivated. Overall, the business will experience increases sales and profits.

> **TOP TIP**
>
> See the page 59 for a full description of the Equality Act 2010.

Quick Fire Questions

1.	What is meant by fair trade?
2.	Give two examples of Fairtrade products.
3.	Outline one disadvantage and one benefit of Fairtrade.
4.	What is meant by ethical behaviour?
5.	Outline one benefit to a business from using ethical operations.

Environmental issues

Caring for the environment is now a huge issue for all businesses, covering such areas as pollution, recycling, waste reduction, omission of greenhouse gases and sustainable development. There are laws in place to cover some of these issues, but businesses have to respond to customers wishes that the environment is not damaged in the production of goods and services.

Environmental issues that businesses **must avoid:**

*   **pollution:** smoke, fumes, gases, emissions into the air

*   **dumping of waste:** waste must be recycled and disposed of carefully and lawfully
*   **using up limited resources:** where possible sustainable resources should be used.

Business can take the following positive actions.

Recycling

*   Recycling allows waste materials to be reused into new products. This means that the worlds' natural resources have a chance to recover and be renewed.
*   Recycled materials can help to save energy in the production process, as products do not require new raw materials.
*   Recycling helps to protect the environment, as greenhouse gas emissions can be reduced and there is less need to keep mining and quarrying for new raw materials.
*   Recycling also helps to reduce landfill sites. If waste materials are recycled, there is no need to dump them into landfill sites that produce greenhouse gases into the environment.

Reducing packaging

Packaging is really important for the final product in any industry. Packaging helps to protect the product during transportation and also to help protect it while on the shelves. Packaging also helps to sell the product if it is a luxury item, like perfume and makeup. However, reducing unnecessary packaging will cut down on waste and therefore the need for more recycling.

Reducing energy

Reducing running costs and energy will also help the environment, as well as business profits. Cutting out additional lighting and heating, reducing vehicle journeys, and avoiding duplication of processes will go a long way towards reducing the damaging effects on the environment.

Analysis of ethical and environmental actions

Businesses that adopt ethical and environmental practices do so because they believe the benefits will outweigh the costs. The costs and benefits are summarised in the table below.

Advantages	Disadvantages
Business will gain a good image and positive reputation, which will attract customers and therefore increase sales and profits. 	Costs of recycling and avoiding dumping of waste. 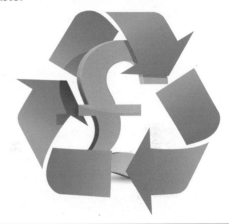
Employees will be more satisfied and motivated if they believe the business is operating in the right way. 	Training and re-training staff to follow ethical and environmental practices. 

Quick Fire Questions

1. Outline two actions that businesses should avoid in order to help the environment.
2. How does recycling help the environment?
3. Explain how reducing packaging and energy helps businesses and the environment.

Technology in marketing and operations 1

Computer-aided design (CAD)

Computer-aided design (CAD) is the name given to software programs that allow the user to create drawings, plans and blueprints using computers. Architects, graphic designers, engineers and designers can produce drawings of potential projects, such as kitchens, bathrooms, houses, bridges, etc. The software allows zooming in and out and viewing the drawings at different angles. Also, if a change is made to a particular aspect of the drawing, all other aspects can be automatically updated. CAD software can now run on PCs and desktop computers. Professional results can be obtained very quickly.

Computer-aided manufacture

Computer-aided manufacture (CAM) is the name given to manufacturing systems that are automated. The production processes are controlled by a computer that can give precise instructions to machines and robots in the production process. CAM is used extensively in the electronics industry. It is hugely beneficial to the business because of the speed, accuracy and continuity of the machinery and equipment. The use of CAM has often led to a reduction in the number of employees required in a business.

Electronic point of sale (EPOS)

EPOS is short for electronic point of sale. This is the system that is used in major retailers at the point where customers pay for their goods. It is often called an 'electronic checkout'. The EPOS system scans the barcodes on the products, which looks up the price of the item and deducts the item from the total stock balance. A receipt is given to the customer, with all the details of the purchase listed along with other information such as special offers, discount vouchers, etc.

EPOS can be used both for market research and stock control. For market research purposes, EPOS can gather information very quickly about the shopping habits of customers. The computer can rank the most popular products sold in a day, week, month, etc. It can also total how much is being spent on each item. This very quickly allows the retailer to make decisions on which products to re-stock quickly.

For stock control purposes, EPOS makes stock recording and stock movements very easy. Each item that is scanned at the point of sale is automatically deducted from the total in stock. The computer can generate stock reports to show which items are nearing their re-order level, and which items have sold the most, or the quickest. All the information is available from the database that is 'behind' the stock system. EPOS can also be used by customers accessing the business' website to see if certain items are in stock (for example, Argos or Ikea). Goods can then be held for customers to uplift from the store or they can be delivered to their homes.

TOP TIP

The use of technology in retailing has changed the way in which businesses interact with their customers. The amount of information available is vast, and consumer behaviour is closely monitored.

Quick Fire Questions

1. What is meant by CAD?
2. What are the advantages of using CAM?
3. Explain how EPOS can be used for stock control.
4. Explain how EPOS can be used for marketing.
5. How can customers benefit from EPOS systems at home?

Technology in marketing and operations 2

Electronic surveys are growing in popularity. More and more businesses and organisations are gathering market research information online. Electronic surveys can be carried out in the following ways:

- sending emails to customers asking for replies to certain questions
- feedback forms on websites
- sending SMS messages, asking for customers to provide ratings
- using survey websites such as Survey Monkey.

This is more immediate and cost-effective than sending out paper questionnaires by post. They are often included as 'pop ups' on a website. The results of the survey can be analysed online and the information is gathered quickly. Designing an electronic survey is easy and the person replying can choose when they do it. There are some concerns, however, that privacy can be breached, or that there are too many surveys so customers will disregard them. There is no guarantee that emails will be read on time or sometimes even read at all. There can also be technical issues with different software and hardware. There is no guarantee that the sample from an electronic survey will be representative of the population.

Online advertising

Businesses can advertise via their own websites, but also through hyperlinks from other websites and through search engines. The main advantages of advertising on the Internet are outlined below:

- a global audience can be reached very quickly
- online advertisements are sophisticated with sound and graphics
- customers can be reached in many ways, for example through tablets, smartphones, iPads
- social networking sites give advertisers opportunities to target specific groups
- customers can be targeted for recommended purchases depending on what they have bought in the past.

Internet-based direct sales

Businesses can choose to sell their products through a distribution channel and third parties or they can sell directly to customers. The use of Internet direct sales has grown rapidly over the last ten years. Large businesses can now sell directly to customers and have the goods delivered straight to their homes. Large online retailers such as Amazon sell their own products as well as branded products. Customers experience rapid delivery times as well as lower prices. The business saves costs on high street outlets and staff.

Targeted online advertising

With the increased use of the Internet, businesses now target customers with advertising. Browsing history can be traced through the use of cookies, which means that adverts can be tailored to the preferences of the user. So browsing one particular website can mean that an advert for that business will appear on another website or search engine. One of the ways that this is done is through 'AdChoices'. The AdChoices icon appears on the browser screen to let the user know that information is being gathered about their interests, and therefore what other adverts they may be interested in. However there is a choice to switch off this option.

AdChoices ▷

Other online retailers also keep a note of purchases from their website and follow this up with recommended purchases. Amazon, for example, sends follow up emails to purchasers recommending other products to purchase based on the original sale. Amazon also highlights this on their website when just browsing. For example, when you are looking at books, DVDs, CDs, etc. Amazon highlights what other customers also viewed.

Electronic viral marketing

Viral marketing is when information about a product or a business gets passed around very quickly from one person to the next, with a snowball effect. With the Internet and electronic communications, this is even more prolific. Text messages, emails, mpegs and YouTube videos can be passed on and spread with incredible speed. Social media such as Facebook and Twitter can also spread the marketing message very effectively. Businesses are aware of the power of this exposure, so aim to tap into this as much as they possibly can, to try and increase awareness of their product/s.

Quick Fire Questions

1. Outline two ways of carrying out an electronic survey.
2. Outline two drawbacks of an electronic survey.
3. Give one advantage to customers from Internet direct sales.
4. Outline two advantages to a business from targeted online advertising.
5. Explain the term 'electronic viral marketing'.

Sample Examination Question

It is becoming more popular to purchase products online. Explain the advantages to an organisation of selling products over the Internet.

4 marks

Answers to questions

Page 17 Quick Fire Questions

1 An entrepreneur creates a business whereas a manager sustains the business.

2 Land is all the natural resources used from the Earth. Labour is the human element or the workers. Capital is machinery and equipment as well as money. Enterprise is the person who has the idea for the business.

3 Wealth is created at each stage of the production process by adding value to that stage.

4 Primary sector involves businesses which extract raw materials from the Earth. Secondary sector involves manufacturing raw materials into finished products. Tertiary sector provides services such as health and retail. Quaternary sector involves knowledge-based and scientific services.

Page 19 Quick Fire Questions

1 Features of a plc are: owned by shareholders, managed by a board of directors, directors are appointed by shareholders at the AGM, shareholders receive dividends on their shares.

2 Dividends

3 Advantages – shareholders have limited liability, more sources of finance available, economies of scale, increased power in the market. Disadvantages – accounts have to be published, shares can be purchased by anyone, has to abide by Companies Act, significant start-up costs.

4 McDonalds, Pizza Hut, Burger King, Body Shop, Dominos.

5 A multinational company is a business that operates in more than one country.

Page 19 Sample Examination Questions

1 The advantages of operating an a franchise are that the franchisee is able to start a business fairly quickly with an established reputation and customer base. They will benefit from the ideas of other franchisees. They will benefit from economies of scale in terms of cheaper advertising, transport costs.

2 The main characteristics of a multinational corporation are that they operate in more than one country. They usually have headquarters in the 'home country' and operate in 'host countries'. They are very large organisations with a range of staff and expertise. They make use of up-to-date technology and equipment in order to communicate around the world. They offer a wide range of quality products at cheaper prices.

3 Multinationals increase living standards by allowing the host country to access jobs and products and services, however the multinational can be very powerful and can make demands on the host country. Multinationals pay taxes in the country where they earn profits, however they can force smaller local businesses to close. Multinationals can learn from their host country in terms of cultures and customs, however they can pull out of the country at any time leaving the host country without jobs.

Page 21 Quick Fire Questions

1 For example, health and defence

2 For example, education and leisure

3 BBC

4 Voluntary organisations are run by volunteers who are interested in the organisation and what it is aiming to do (e.g. Scouts, Guides, local football teams), whereas a charity is interested in raising funds for good causes and has both volunteers and paid employees.

5 Social Enterprises are different from other third sector organisations as they are run in a business like way and have a specific aim (e.g. a social or environmental aim). Their employees get paid in the usual way.

Page 21 Sample Examination Question

1 Organisations in the private sector are owned and controlled by private individuals, whereas organisations in the public sector are collectively owned by everyone, and third sector organisations are not owned by anyone. Private sector organisations aim to make a profit, whereas public sector organisations aim to cover their costs, and third sector organisations aim to raise money for good causes. Private sector organisations raise finance from private individuals, whereas public sector organisations raise finance from taxes, and third sector organisations raise finance from donations, government grants, and lottery funding.

Page 23 Quick Fire Questions

1 Objectives are targets or goals that an organisation sets for itself and these are usually expressed in terms of a mission statement. The mission statement will set out how the business intends to achieve these targets and goals.

2 Private sector objectives include making a profit, whereas public sector and third sector are not-for-profit organisations.

3 Businesses may wish to grow in order to increase their market share, to gain economies of scale, and to make sure of their continued survival in the market.

4 Horizontal integration is when two businesses at the same stage of production join together (e.g. two banks become one), whereas vertical integration is when two businesses at different stages in the production process become one (e.g. a supermarket buys over the farm which provides them with fruit and vegetables).

5 A merger is when two businesses agree to become one company.

Page 23 Sample Examination questions

1 An organisation can have conflicting objectives as they may aim to make a profit, but also want to keep their customers happy. If customers want low prices this will conflict with the profit objective.

2 Possible methods of growth for a plc are: vertical integration where two businesses at different stages in the production process merge; horizontal integration where two businesses at the same stage of the production process merge; a merger where two businesses agree to become one; a takeover where one business buys over another; diversification where two businesses in completely different types of production join together; organic growth where a business opens more branches, takes on more employees, etc and grows naturally.

3 Horizontal integration – firms producing the same products combine together. This allows for greater economies of scale, which allows for lower unit costs and increased profits. By becoming larger, they should become better known in the market and this should lead to brand loyalty and increased sales. They might dominate the market due to the greater size of the organisation and can then set prices and encourage customers to purchase from them through large promotional activities. By removing competitors, they will increase sales. Vertical integration – firms at different stages in the production process combine together. This can cut out middle men and allow the organisation to retain all profits made in the chain themselves. Backward vertical – when a firm combines with a supplier, which ensures that there is constant and consistent supplies of raw materials at appropriate prices. Forward vertical – when a firm combines with a customer which ensures that sales are constant and can increase profits. Conglomerate/diversification – when a firm combines with another firm in a completely different market. This means that profits can be made from a variety of markets and sales do not rely on just one industry.

Page 27 Quick Fire Questions

1 A wide span of control is when a manager has a large number of employees under their command, whereas a narrow span of control is when a manger has a small number of employees under their command.

2 Chain of command – where instructions are passed down from one level to another in an organisation. Responsibility – answerable for decisions and actions taken. Delegate – someone requests a task to be done by a sub-ordinate. Functional grouping – grouping by department.

3 A benefit of customer grouping is that goods and services can be targeted directly to the needs of customers in that group.

4 Businesses may group according to city, or council (e.g. East Ayrshire, Morayshire) or by international country (e.g. Italy, France).

Page 27 Sample Examination Questions

1 The effects of increasing a manager's span of control are complex. The manager may experience stress, as the number of employees they are in charge of increases. The manager might feel they do not have enough time to supervise the employee properly. The employees might feel they do not have the proper support from their manager. Employees may resent having to make decisions and may not have the confidence to do so. However, employees may feel more empowered as they will have more tasks delegated to them and they can make their own decisions. Employees may not feel that managers are closely supervising them and this gives them more freedom.

2 Customer grouping can easily build up loyalty. There is a high level of customer care and the organisation can respond to the customer needs quickly. It can be expensive due to high staffing costs to meet customer needs. New staff are needed if there is a new customer grouping or product created. Competition between customer groupings/departments can exist.

3 Staff with similar expertise work together in functional grouping but in product grouping staff are organised around a specific product or service and will have different areas of expertise. The organisation will have functional departments which service the whole organisation, whereas in product grouping each functional area will be responsible for a specific product or service only. In both methods, departments can be more concerned with their own results than the organisation as a whole. Also, departments may compete against each other in both forms of grouping. In product grouping it is easier to identify areas that are performing well, whereas in functional

grouping results tend to be for the organisation as a whole. In product grouping each department is more responsive to change, but in functional grouping the organisation can become very large and unresponsive. In functional grouping staff will know exactly who to turn to, but in product grouping this may not be the case. In functional grouping the organisation will have a clear structure, but in product grouping the structure may be less clear and line relationships less clear.

Page 31 Quick Fire Questions

1   Hierarchical structure has many layers of management, whereas flat structure has few layers of management.

2   A matrix structure would be formed for a specific reason, e.g. to work on a particular project.

3   An entrepreneurial structure would be found in smaller oganisations.

4   A centralised structure is associated with a hierarchical structure.

5   A decentralised structure allows decisions to be made across all levels in the organisation, although this tends to be flat structures.

6   A business may wish to restructure to keep with up the changing business environment or to respond to external factors.

7   Delayering is when an organisation removes levels of management, downsizing is when an organisation reduces the scale of its operations across the whole organisation, and outsourcing is when an organisation sends some of its core activities out to another organisation to do on their behalf.

Page 31 Sample Examination Questions

1   In a decentralised structure decision making is delegated to departments, whereas in a centralised structure decision making lies with senior managers. A decentralised structure relieves senior managers of a lot of the daily tasks, but in a centralised structure managers carry the whole burden of decision making. In a decentralised structure subordinates are given responsibility to make decisions (which is motivational), whereas in a centralised structure subordinates are less motivated as decision making is made only by senior managers. In a decentralised structure decision making is faster than in a centralised structure, as local managers do not have to consult national managers prior to making a decision. In a centralised structure procedures tend to be standardised throughout the organisation, but in a decentralised structure procedures will be decided by local managers. In a centralised structure decisions are taken for the organisation as a whole, whereas in a decentralised structure decisions take into account local arrangements/customers. In a centralised structure a high degree of corporate identity exists, whereas in a decentralised structure corporate culture is harder to impose.

2   In an entrepreneurial structure one senior member of staff makes all the important decisions. Decisions are therefore made quickly. Staff are very rarely consulted on decision making. It stifles staff initiative as they are not consulted. The employees know who they are accountable to, but it may place over-reliance on key members of staff.

3   In delayering, a complete level of management is cut out, which will reduce the salaries paid out by the organisation. Managers have an increased span of control, which may result in increased workload for the manager. There may be increased stress for the manager. The staff have to wait to meet with a manager. Communication should be improved and be quicker to pass on, which means the organisation will be more receptive to changes in the marketplace. Empowers the staff which can lead to increased motivation. However, fewer promotion opportunities for staff could lead to them leaving to gain promotion.

Page 33 Quick Fire Questions

1   Finance – businesses must have access to the finance they need to run the business properly. Lack of finance can lead to problems. Employees – need to be correctly qualified and trained for the jobs they do, otherwise customers will not be happy. Management – must be able to make good quality decisions on behalf of the business. Existing technology – the business must embrace technology in order to stay competitive.

2   Corporate culture is the overall impression that the business gives to customers and employees. It is about achieving objectives overall.

3   Corporate culture can be achieved by staff wearing uniforms, having a corporate style (e.g. logo, colours, mascot). It can also be achieved by team building activities and good customer service.

Page 33 Sample Examination Question

1   The organisation needs to take into account the ideas/principles of the owners. They need to design appropriate logos, motifs and uniforms. They need to consider a corporate design for shops and outlets. They have to make staff aware of the corporate culture and image, but this can be expensive and may involve staff training costs. The organisation may decide to hold launch events or press conferences. The organisation should have clearly defined policies and procedures.

Page 35 Quick Fire Questions

1   Planning – Looking at future needs of the organisation. Organisation – Ensuring necessary resources will be available. Commanding – Instructing others in what needs to be done. Coordinating – Making sure there is joined up thinking. Controlling – Overseeing developments. Delegating – Entrusting tasks to others. Motivating – Encouraging staff to achieve their potential.

2   Strategic – Long term decisions made by senior management. Tactical – Medium term decisions made by senior and middle managers. Operational – Everyday decisions which are made by junior managers.

3   Factors which could affect the quality or effectiveness of decisions include: the experience and skills of the manager, the data or information available, the time allowed to make the decision, the commitment of those who will implement the decisions.

4   Strengths include strong market share, finance available, highly qualified and skilled staff. Weaknesses include out-of-date technology, finance problems, lack of motivated staff.

Page 37 Quick Fire Questions

1   Political factors include the government passing new laws regarding health and safety, working conditions or taxation.

2   Economics factors include recession, unemployment, competition.

3   Social changes that influence demand include fashion and taste changes, or changes in population structure (e.g. more old people).

4   Changes in technology include mobile phones, tablet computers, social network sites.

5   A business can become more socially responsible by recycling and caring for the environment.

Page 37 Sample Examination Question

1 Legislation – any new law passed by the government can have an impact on the organisation as they will have to comply with that law, and this usually costs them money. Taxation rates may change which will affect the profitability of an organisation. The government may introduce new finance schemes for business loans and grants, and this can have a positive effect on business finance. The government may introduce new policies which impact on the business (e.g. education and training for employees).

Page 40 Quick Fire Questions

1 Businesses will find it harder to secure funds for growth.

2 Austerity means that businesses and individuals have less money to spend, therefore there is reduced demand for goods and services.

3 Low interest rates encourages individuals to spend rather than save.

4 It increases economic growth.

Page 40 Sample Examination Question

1 Competition policy can assist and prevent businesses from achieving their objectives, depending on the policy being introduced. The EU allows businesses to achieve growth however it can lead to further competition from abroad. Other elements of competition policy prevent businesses from setting high prices, which reduce the amount of profit they can make. Mergers and takeovers can sometimes be blocked by the government which reduces opportunities for growth.

Page 43 Quick Fire Questions

1 Stakeholders are: employees, managers, owners, customers, government, local community, suppliers and pressure groups.

2 Interdependence of stakeholders means that both sides are prepared to work together and compromise in order to achieve their objectives.

3 Conflict between stakeholders arises when their aims are directly at odds with each other.

4 Conflict between stakeholders may be resolved by the stakeholder with the greatest influence getting their own way, or the stakeholder with the greatest impact getting their own way.

Page 46 Quick Fire Questions

1 Workforce planning is when businesses plan their workforce requirements in order to meet their strategic objectives.

2 Internal recruitment is when existing employees are appointed to new positions within the business, whereas external recruitment is when new employees are brought in from outside the business.

3 A job description outlines the duties and responsibilities of the job, whereas a person specification clarifies the skills and qualities required from the person doing the job.

4 Newspaper, internet website, job centres.

5 A recruitment agency can be used to provide a suitable shortlist of candidates for interview, or they can carry out assessments of potential candidates.

Page 46 Sample Examination Question

1 Identify a job vacancy, conduct a job analysis, prepare a job description, prepare a person specification, advertise the vacancy.

Page 49 Quick Fire questions

1 Interview, asking candidates to make a presentation, role play, group interviews, team building tasks, assessments or testing.

2 Recruitment is the process of getting potential candidates to apply for the job and usually includes the point of receiving completed applications. Thereafter, selection involves sifting through the applications and selecting candidates to be interviewed or tested.

3 During team building and group discussion activities 'natural leaders' can emerge. Candidates can be assessed on how they interact with others.

4 Personality can be tested by asking about thoughts and feelings, whereas aptitude is tested by literacy, numeracy, problem-solving and reasoning tasks.

5 Group exercises, in-tray exercises, presentations, case studies, psychometric testing, social activities.

6 This is when an employee is taken on for an agreed period of time, so that they can be assessed on their performance during that time. If they are satisfactory, they will usually be kept on.

Page 49 Sample Examination Questions

1 Compare application forms and CVs with the person specification to make sure candidates meet the criteria. Interview the candidates to find out about their personalities and skills. Ask the candidates to take part in presentations, group discussions, role play, etc in order to assess their personalities and skills. Use an assessment centre to test and interview the candidates.

2 Interviews are used to gather information on potential employees' abilities. They allow the organisation to compare candidates in a pressure situation. They give the candidates a chance to respond to questions. The interviewers can compare notes to get a consensus on who the best candidate was. Interview styles can change, allowing the organisation to examine potential candidates under different situations (i.e. long leet and short leet interviews, group interviews, presentations).

3   Attainment – a candidate is given the chance to demonstrate their skills, e.g. it would be used to test skills in ICT or to measure skills against a set standard. Aptitude – assesses a candidate's personal abilities and skills, e.g. it would be used to decide if the candidate had the required skills and aptitude for a job, (i.e. numerical skills for an accounts vacancy). Intelligence/ IQ – measures a candidate's mental ability, e.g. it is used for jobs where candidates may be solving problems. Psychometric/psychological – assesses a candidate's personality and can be used to assess the candidate's mental suitability for a job. Medical – measures a candidate's physical attributes and is used for jobs such as the fire brigade that require certain levels of physical strength.

Page 52 Quick Fire Questions

1   On-the-job, off-the-job and induction training.

2   For example, lectures, role play, job rotation, apprenticeships, multimedia.

3   Higher skilled more effective employees leads to reductions in customer complaints. Higher skilled more effective employees leads to reductions in absenteeism and staff turnover. Higher skilled more effective employees will be ambitious and will apply for vacancies, therefore reducing the skills gap.

4   Graduate training and vocational training.

5   Disadvantages are: The finance required for computers and other equipment. Some employees do not like to learn in a VLE and they may be more comfortable learning in a more traditional way. If the internet or network system is down employees are unable to access the VLE which can lead to delays in completing their training. Benefits are: Employees do not have to lose time away from their jobs in order to be trained. Travel costs are reduced and the costs of paying lecturers and trainers is also reduced. Employees will feel more motivated if they have training opportunities, and will produce better quality work as their skills improve.

Page 52 Sample Examination Questions

1   Staff training allows for a wider pool of skills to be available to the organisation, so staff can carry out a wider range of tasks and cover for absent colleagues. Staff training is motivational for staff and should mean they are happier at their work, which will improve performance. Staff training can improve the quality of product/service provided, which will result in improved customer relations. It improves the image of the organisation, which means they will attract a better calibre of worker and therefore more people wishing to work for them. It should reduce the number of accidents at work, which will reduce any compensation or injuries to employees/customers. It may be required to introduce change and will make the staff more acceptable to change.

2   Costs of staff training are: hiring of 'experts' to deliver the training, costs of hiring venue for training to take place, costs of covering for employees who are away from the work place, possible lack of continuity with customers when employees are being trained, costs of travel expenses for employees.

Page 55 Quick Fire Questions

1   Taylor's theory: when employees are only interested in money; Mayo's theory: when employees need more than just money at work; Maslow's hierarchy of needs; Herzberg's theory of motivators and hygiene factors.

2   A democratic leader consults with employees before making decisions, allows employees to use their initiative, and delegates to employees.

3   A financial reward is direct payment; non-financial rewards are additional benefits, e.g. company car, pension, staff discount, etc.

4   Rewards help to motivate employees as they feel valued, and if they work harder it will be to their own benefit.

5   Financial rewards are paid by time rates, piece rates, overtime, salary or bonus. Non-financial rewards are company car, pension, luncheon vouchers, staff discount, child care vouchers.

Page 55 Sample Examination Questions

1   Use of staff training to motivate staff. Give bonuses or financial rewards. Make use of profit sharing schemes. Organise team building days or social events. Have staff involvement in works councils/quality circles. Have regular consultation with staff. Job enlargement or enrichment schemes. However, all of these involve time and money, which can result in the business losing profits.

2   With time rate workers are paid per hour, but in piece rate they are paid for the amount of items they produce. Both time rate and piece rate are mainly used in manual jobs. Time rate is simple to calculate, whereas piece rate is harder to calculate due to the amount per item calculation. Piece rate is an incentive to produce more items, whereas time rate is an incentive to work longer hours. Both systems can sacrifice quality for output, if workers work more hours or try to produce more products.

3   Commission – This is a reward for the amount of a product or service sold to customers. It can be paid on top of a basic salary, or paid as a percentage of the product's sale value.

Overtime – This is normal hourly rate plus an increase for extra hours worked. It can be paid at a higher rate, and is an incentive to work more than the contracted hours.

Bonus rate – Employees are paid a basic rate with a bonus on top for meeting agreed targets. It is an incentive to produce more or work harder.

Page 57 Quick Fire Questions

1   Employee relations involves encouraging and motivating staff to develop and perform to their potential in their job. It also involves communicating, negotiating and bargaining with staff on a more official basis through Trade Unions and Works Councils.

2   Counselling, stress management, return to work interviews, family friendly policies.

3   Employees will be motivated if they have good facilities and places to relax at work.

4   Appraisals allow employees to focus on working towards pay increases, promotion or training and development.

5   Employees may not perform to their highest level which affects customers. The business might find it difficult to attract good quality staff.

Page 57 Sample Examination Questions

1   Employees may be set appropriate targets, and staff training could be given in order to allow these targets to be met. Positive feedback could be given to the employee during appraisal meetings. Support systems could be put into place, e.g. counselling. Regular meetings could be held with their line manager or a mentor appointed.

2   De-motivated workforce may result in: decreased productivity, increased staff turnover, increased staff absenteeism, impact on the quality of output, and less co-operation of staff during periods of change could make it harder to introduce new policies or procedures.

Page 59 Quick Fire Questions

1   The purpose of a trade union is to help its members secure the best pay and working conditions possible.

2   Strike – when employees refuse to go to work. Overtime-ban – when employees refuse to work extra hours. Sit-in – when employees occupy the building. Work to rule – when employees only do exactly what their contract says. Go slow – when employees still do their job but much more slowly than normal.

3   Employers provide and maintain safety equipment and safe systems of work; ensure materials used are properly stored, handled, used and transported; provide information, training, instruction and supervision; provide a safe place of employment, e.g. fire extinguishers, protective clothing, have health and safety representatives.

4   The Equality Act 2010 ensures that everyone is treated fairly at work regardless of their race, religion, gender, disability etc. The Minimum Wage Act ensures that employees get a fair wage.

Page 59 Sample Examination Questions

1   The features of the Equality Act 2010 are fair and equal treatment for all employees and removal of discrimination. Potential candidates and existing employees cannot be discriminated on the grounds of: sex, race, marital status, religion, disability, sexual orientation or pregnancy. Employees must be provided with the necessary support to carry out their jobs correctly, e.g. accessible buildings.

2   Strike – when employees refuse to go to work and do not get paid. There has to be a ballot of all members before this can take place. Overtime-ban – when employees refuse to work extra hours which can have a negative effect on customer orders. Sit-in – when employees occupy the building which prevents normal work from taking place. Work to rule – when employees only do exactly what their contract says and nothing extra. This can damage goodwill with management. Go slow – when employees still do their job but much more slowly than normal which therefore affects output.

Page 62 Quick Fire Questions

1   Monitor and control of expenses – The role of the Finance Function is to monitor and control expenses to make sure that the organisation does not end up in financial difficulty. Forecast future financial information – They forecast future financial information by performing 'what if' scenarios. Check on performance – They check on performance by preparing financial statements and ratio analysis and comparing with other businesses. Provide information for decision-making – They provide information for decision-making by producing reports and statistics. Monitor cash flow – They monitor cash flow by preparing cash budgets so that the business does not overspend.

2   An employee would be interested to see if their job is secure; the owner to judge how successful the business is; a shareholder to see if they are going to continue to invest in the business; the general public to see how secure the business is for employment; a supplier to see if they will get paid on time.

3   HMRC – which is Her Majesty's Revenue and Customs. This organisation collects taxes.

4   A lender would want to make sure that the business was in a secured position, so that they are assured that their money will be paid back to them.

Page 64 Quick Fire Questions

1   Positive cash flow is important because if the business does not have enough cash to operate it can go into liquidation.

2   Balance means total.

3   Surplus is a positive closing balance, whereas deficit is a negative closing balance.

4   Increase sales revenue, reduce expenses, spread purchase of assets.

5   Cash flow is total amount of cash received, whereas profit is the difference between the cost of goods sold and sales revenue.

6   Rent, wages, gas, electricity, petrol, etc.

Page 64 Sample Examination Questions

1   The finance department must ensure that corporation tax is accurate, PAYE must be calculated for all employees, VAT must be returned regularly and they must have good record keeping.

2   Customers being given too long a credit period. Customers being given too high a credit limit. Owners taking out too much money through drawings, and having high debts with increased rates of interest. Suppliers not allowing credit or very short credit period. Sales revenue not high enough. Sudden increase in expenses. Capital expenditure, e.g. purchase of machinery.

3   Use marketing measures to move unwanted stock. Reduce the length of time given to customers to pay for goods. Have a maximum amount owners can withdraw/reduce drawings. Try to get increased credit terms. Find a cheaper supplier. Reduce wages/expenses. Take out a short term overdraft. Increase owners' own capital. Reduce repayment of loans.

4   Cash budgets highlight periods when cash flow will be a problem. They can be used to secure loans or to show investors, and are used to make comparisons between actual expenditure and targeted. They can show periods that the organisation will have cash available for major investment or purchases of fixed assets. They are used to give departments a budget to focus on (targets), and are used to monitor spending throughout the organisation.

Page 67 Quick Fire Questions

1   Trading and Profit and Loss Account and Balance Sheet.

2   Sales less cost of sales

3   Gross profit less expenses

4   Wages, electricity, gas, advertising, etc

5   Fixed assets examples are buildings, machinery, equipment which all last for a long time. Current assets examples are stock, debtors, bank and cash. They do not last for a long time.

Page 67 Sample Examination Question

1   Shareholders could look at any ratios calculated, e.g. gross profit %. Trading account shows the profit and loss made from buying and selling stock over a period of time. Profit and loss account shows the overall profit or loss over a specified time period. Balance sheet which shows the financial position of a business at an exact moment in time. Cash budgets show projected income and expenditure for the following year. Share prices show the current value of the organisation.

Page 71 Quick Fire Questions

1   This is bad as it is below the average for the industry. The business will want to find out the reasons why their figure is below average.

2   Increase sales revenue, reduce cost of sales, improve stock management.

3   Gross profit figure is found in the trading account.

4   Increase in the gross profit %, reduction in expenses.

Page 71 Sample Examination Questions

1   The information is historical and the findings do not take into account external factors. New products or product development is not taken into account. Staff morale or turnover is not taken into account, and you can't compare with different organisations, as you do not know the basis used, e.g. stock valuations. It assumes the information they are based on is reliable.

2   **Current ratio: current assets/current liabilities**, answer of 2:1 is the accepted ratio. Allows managers to monitor liquidity levels of the business and shows the ability to pay short term debts. **Acid test ratio: current assets – stock/current liabilities**, 1:1 is the accepted ratio. Allows managers to know that they can pay off debts quickly. **Gross profit ratio: gross profit/ sales × 100** measures the percentage profit made from buying and selling stock. Can be used by managers to compare to the industry standard. **Net profit ratio: net profit/sales × 100** measures the percentage profit after expenses have been paid. Can be used by managers to control expenses or analyse expenses. **ROCE: net profit/opening capital × 100** measures the return on capital for investors in a business. Can be compared to other organisations or a safe investment such as using a building society to invest in. **Mark up: gross profit/cost of goods sold × 100** measures how much is added to the cost of goods for profit. Used to ensure a satisfactory level of profit is made. **Rate of stock turnover: cost of goods sold/average stock**, is used to analyse how quickly the stock is sold and is useful for sales of perishable items.

Page 74 Quick Fire Questions

1   Large sums of money can be generated from selling shares.

2   A grant does not have to be paid back whereas a loan does.

3   There is no initial outlay when leasing, whereas buying the asset there is usually a large initial outlay.

4   Debts are sold to a third party who then tries to recoup the debt.

Page 74 Sample Examination Question

1   Finance brings in additional capital from the owners which doesn't have to be repaid. Bank loan – over a period of time paid back (in instalments) with interest, it allows for the payments to be spread out. Bank overdraft – a smaller amount for shorter period of time borrowed from bank, it is useful when only needed for a short period of time and is relatively easy to arrange. Grant – might be possible to receive a government grant under certain conditions, it does not have to be paid back. Retained profits from previous years – does not involve any re-payments or interest. Venture capital – provides finance when banks thinks it is too risky – often good for riskier investments or ideas. Mortgage – used to purchase buildings over a long period of time therefore easy to manage.

Page 75 Quick Fire Questions

1   Software applications are used to record and process business documents, financial transactions and to store and retrieve data.

2   Payroll, track credit transactions, produce cash budgets and financial statements.

3   Dedicated software can have specialised reports built into the software to suit the business.

4   Graphs can highlight trends and variances very quickly.

5   Costs of purchasing the hardware and software, costs of maintenance and security, technical support and training.

Page 77 Quick Fire Questions

1   Customer segments are: age, gender, income, social class, cultural, geographical location, education and family lifestyle.

2   Consumer behaviour is influenced by personality, time of year, family events, economic factors, e.g. recession. It is also influenced by routine purchases, e.g. bread and milk.

Page 77 Sample Examination Question

1   Product-led businesses concentrate on their product as they believe the product is good quality and will always sell. They do not undertake extensive market research. However market-led businesses conduct extensive market research to amend and update their products based on what customers want.

Page 79 Quick Fire Questions

1   Who are the customers? What is their age group? What prices are they willing to pay? This information can be used to improve effectiveness as the business will know exactly who to target and how. They will also be able to set prices accurately.

2   Bias on the part of the interviewer, unreliable information or inaccurate responses.

3   Random sampling, quota sampling, systematic sampling, convenience sampling.

4   When deciding on a sample, the business should take into account the type of product, the location of the business, the stage of the product life cycle.

Page 79 Sample Examination Question

1   Quota sampling involves selecting certain groups of the population that meet certain criteria or market segments, whereas random sampling involves choosing anyone from the population at random.

Page 81 Quick Fire Questions

1   Personal interview, technology survey, consumer panel, hall test, observation.

2   Disadvantages – It is very expensive to carry out as researchers have to be employed. It is very time-consuming to collect. In order to obtain meaningful results large numbers have to be interviewed. Benefits – The information gathered is relevant. The information is accurate and reliable. The information can be kept private from competitors.

3   Using government data, printed media, e.g. books, journals, online research.

4   Disadvantages – The information may not be relevant to your business. The information may not always be accurate or up-to-date or totally reliable. The information is freely available to competitors so it is not always helpful in gaining a competitive edge. Benefits – The information is relatively cheap to obtain. The information is usually easy to obtain. It is useful for analysing past trends in the market and therefore predicting future trends.

Page 81 Sample Examination Questions

1   Personal interview/questionnaire/survey – This can be done in different ways, e.g. face-to-face on the street, telephone survey, written questionnaire. Technology survey – New technology allows customers to give personal feedback on websites or using mobile phones. Consumer panel/focus group – This is when a group of customers is brought together to discuss a product or service.

Hall test – This involves giving a free sample or trial of a product to a group of customers and they are asked to give their opinion once they have tried it out. Observation – A lot of information can be gathered by observing customers.

2   Telephone surveys – used by organisations to call customers and gain their views. Instant feedback can be given. Postal survey – where questionnaires are posted out to customers who complete them and return them to the organisations. Could send these out to all customers, or customers in selected areas, gaining their opinions. Personal interview – where people are stopped in the street and asked questions, it can clarify any questions to aid understanding, and allows two-way communication.

Page 85 Quick Fire Questions

1   Research – This is when research and development of the product take place. This involves developing a prototype and test marketing in order to get feedback from customers. Introduction – This is when the product is introduced or launched onto the market. Growth – Once customers know about the product sales begin to grow. Maturity – At this stage everyone who wants the product has already purchased it and sales level out. Saturation – At the very end of the maturity stage the product is saturated as no further growth is possible. Decline – Sales of the product start to fall as there are no new customers.

2   Any two strategies from the 7Ps – Product, Price, Place, Promotion, People, Process and Physical Evidence.

3   This is when a business has more than one product in their range to sell.

4   Benefits – Customers will already know the existing product lines therefore new ones can be introduced quickly. Risk of failure is spread across a range of products. Market share can be increased as different products will appeal to different market segments. Disadvantages – If there is a problem with one product it can affect the reputation of all the products in the line. The business may have to invest heavily in machinery and equipment to make a range of different product lines. The business will continually have to train staff to produce new products in the product line.

5   Virgin, Unilever.

Page 85 Sample Examination Questions

1   Introduction – This is when the product is introduced or launched onto the market. Growth – Once customers know about the product sales begin to grow. Maturity – At this stage everyone who wants the product has already purchased it and sales level out. Decline – Sales of the product start to fall as there are no new customers.

2   Introduction – Profits are low as there are high outlay costs to get the product onto the market. Growth – profits are increasing. Maturity – profits reach their highest level and start to flatten out. Decline – profits start to decrease.

3 Improve the product – this will attract new consumers to purchase the product. Alter the packaging – this may appeal to a different market segment. Increase/decrease the price – price changes can attract new consumers to purchase the product. Use a different or new advertising campaign/advertising media – this will highlight the product in a different manner. Change the use of the product – new use of the product will be popular with different market segments. Introduce line extensions to the product – various product line extensions will appeal to different segments and may increase overall. Alter the place the product is sold – selling the product in a variety of ways will mean a larger number of consumers can purchase the product.

Page 87 Quick Fire Questions

1 What did it cost to make? What price are competitors charging? Is the product sensitive to very small changes in price?

2 High prices are set when the business is confident that consumers will pay it, whereas low prices are set when the business wants to undercut the competition.

3 Cost plus pricing is based on the cost of production plus a percentage profit added on.

4 This is when prices are set just below a certain limit, e.g. £19.99 seems cheaper than £20.

5 They use them to compare prices for the same product or service from a range of different suppliers in order to get the best price.

Page 87 Sample Examination Questions

1 Premium pricing – Choose a high price to sell the product, this will give the customer an image of quality. Market skimming – Start off with a high price to sell the product. This will appeal to a certain market segment who want the product in the introductory stage. Allows the business to make high profits prior to competitors entering the market.

2 High Price – price is set higher than competitors to give the image of quality and exclusiveness. Low Price – price is set lower than competitors to attract customers to their product/service. Skimming – price is set high initially when no competition exists, when competitors enter the market price is lowered to market price. Market/Competitive Pricing – price is set at the same level as competitors, normally used for products that are identical. Penetration Pricing – price is set slightly lower than competitors to attract customers, once a customer base has been created price is slowly increased to same as competitors. Promotional Pricing – a low price is set for a short period of time to boost sales in the short term, possibly even making a loss on the product. Destroyer Pricing – price is set very low compared to competitors, and once there is no competition in the market the price is then put back up to the previous level or higher.

Page 91 Quick Fire Questions

1 Manufacturer to customer, manufacturer to wholesaler to customer, manufacturer to retailer to customer, manufacturer to wholesaler to retailer to customer

2 For customers, the bulk is broken down into small amounts; for small businesses, the wholesaler provides discounts.

3 For the customer, a local place to shop with advice and after sales service; for the manufacturer, a reliable outlet for their products.

4 Road, rail, aeroplane, sea.

5 Cost of the vessel, getting to docks, journey can take a long time.

Page 91 Sample Examination Questions

1 Retailers are located closer to the customer. They often have an established customer base. They can hold stock. Have trained sales staff who are knowledgeable about the products. Will attract customers by offers of credit facilities. Can offer appropriate after sales services. Retailers buy in bulk. Reduced delivery cost. Retailers paying for advertising.

   Products displayed attractively by the retailer.

2 Road – Refrigerated vehicles can be used to transport perishable items; is an easy way to get direct to a customer's location; as road networks improve it is a quick method; can have problems with delays, road works and weather. Cost of fuel rising makes the overall cost dearer. Rail – Ideal for heavy products; is more environmentally friendly than road; requires specialised freight terminals to load products; not suitable in rural areas with no rail network. Air – This is perfect for long distances or more remote areas; is a faster method for overseas distribution; can be more expensive than road or rail. Sea – Ideal when heavy or bulky goods are transported; is good for items that are not time bound; is a slower method than the others.

3 Advantages – Saves the manufacturer from making lots of smaller deliveries, so saves on transport costs. Saves the manufacturer from having high stockholding costs as a lot of the stock is held by the wholesaler. If there are changes in trends and fashions, the manufacturer will not be left with unsold stock. Wholesalers can help label and package the product for the manufacturer, which saves time consuming/less work for the manufacturer.
   Retailers can buy from wholesalers in smaller amounts which can help increase overall sales.
   Disadvantages – By using wholesalers, manufacturers lose control over the image of their product which could mean the product not being presented the way the manufacturer would want. Profits are lost to the wholesaler, which could be kept by the manufacturer improving their financial position.

Page 94 Quick Fire Questions

1 'Into the pipeline' promotions are aimed at retailers and 'out of the pipeline' promotions are aimed at consumers.

2 'Above the line' advertising targets a mass audience, whereas 'below the line' advertising is more targeted.

3 Social media advertising has meant that individuals can now receive targeted advertising directly to their mobile device or tablet.

4 Ethical marketing avoids making claims about products or services which are not true.

5 They can report the advertisement to the ASA – Advertising Standards Authority.

Page 94 Sample Examination Question

1 Television – Large audiences can be targeted at the one time, which allows it to cover all market segments. Products can appear appealing which will attract more customers. High profile can be maintained with regular advertising, which will keep the product in the consumer's mind. Newspapers/Magazines – National or local exposure can be obtained in order to suit the market segment or product. Technical information can be given to customers. Customers can refer back to the advert allowing consumers longer to make purchasing decisions. Radio – Cheaper than television therefore saves the organisation's costs. Can have a captive audience as listeners tend not to change channels if an advert comes on. Billboards/Posters – Can have an excellent visual impact which will last in the consumer's mind; is frequently seen by the same consumer which will enhance the impact. Internet – The use of

links can allow exact markets to be targeted, which should increase the effectiveness of the advert. It is very easy to change adverts on websites, which allows for them to be constantly changed quite cheaply.

Page 99 Quick Fire Questions

1   People, Process and Physical evidence

2   Employees have to be trained to carry out their role properly – the main emphasis is on customer service and customer interaction.

3   Physical state of the building, image of employees, corporate image (e.g. logos, etc), employees in uniform, written policies, etc.

Page 101 Quick Fire Questions

1   'Just in time' stock control means having raw materials delivered as and when they are needed for production.

2   Disadvantages – Suppliers must be reliable for stocks to arrive on time. It can be difficult to respond quickly to changes in demand. Delays in transport or adverse weather conditions can hold up deliveries. Benefits – Avoids warehouse costs or stock room costs, therefore production costs are lower. Avoids deterioration of stock that has not been stored properly. Avoids stocks going out of date or fashion too quickly. Avoids theft or pilfering of stock, therefore improving profit figures.

3   Suppliers must be reliable so that stocks arrive on time. They must be flexible and able to respond quickly to changes in demand.

4   Maximum stock level – This is the highest level of stock that the business will hold in order to minimise costs and make the most efficient use of the space. The level depends on usage and delivery times. Minimum stock level – This is the lowest level that stock should not fall below, in order to make sure that there are no shortages and production does not have to be stopped. The level depends on usage.

5   Warehouse or stock room should be well-lit, dry and well ventilated. A system should be used for booking stock in and out of the warehouse. Stock should be used on a first in, first out basis. Accurate records should be kept of stock levels. Warehouses or stock rooms should be supervised and locked. Appropriate space should be given to stock items. All shelves and storage areas should be labelled for easy access.

Page 101 Sample Examination Questions

1   Understocking – Becomes harder to cope with unexpected changes in demand, which means customers may go elsewhere to purchase the product if the firm doesn't have it in stock. If customers go elsewhere they may lose them completely, and not just the one time. Production may have to stop completely as there are no raw materials to use in production which can mean paying for workers who aren't producing any goods. Overstocking – Carrying large amounts of stock will increase the cost of storage, reducing profit, and may result in having to pay larger insurance costs. Capital is tied up in stock which means that the money cannot be used elsewhere, such as advertising. The stock may deteriorate, resulting in larger wastage costs. Changes in trends and fashion will mean that stock might become obsolete and not be able to be sold.

2 Capital is not tied up in stock and can be used elsewhere in the organisation. There is less warehouse space needed for stock. Less stock is stored which should result in less wastage. Theft will be reduced as stock is more tightly controlled. Changes in fashion or trends will have less of an impact. If stock does not arrive, production can stop. There will be an increase in delivery costs as more frequent transportation exists. There is a high dependence on suppliers.

Page 103 Quick Fire Questions

1 Labour intensive uses mostly humans in the production process; capital intensive uses mostly machines and equipment in the production process.

2 Mechanisation uses machines with people involved; automation is robots and machines doing all the work.

3 Job – piece of furniture or clothing. Batch – bread, cakes, wallpaper. Flow – cars.

4 Advantages – Production costs can be reduced because many products can be made at the same time. There can still be some degree of tailoring the batches to the customers requirements. Disadvantages – Switching between batches can be time consuming if changes to machinery need to be made. If there is a problem with one product in the batch the whole batch may be affected.

5 Advantages – Very large numbers of products can be made quickly at the same time thus lowering unit costs of production. The use of machinery allows the production process to be running constantly (often fully automated). Quality assurance can be built into each stage of the production process. Disadvantages – the product is exactly the same for each customer – there is no tailoring to their requirements. There are very high costs involved for machinery and production lines. There are very little opportunities for employees to use their skills and initiative, as many of the tasks involved are boring and repetitive.

Page 103 Sample Examination Questions

1 Job production – this is usually defined as one 'job' which is done at a time by an individual skilled worker. The job involves a high degree of skill on behalf of the employees and the job can take a long time to complete. Batch production – this is usually defined as groups of products which are made at the same time in batches. Each product in the batch is the same, but there may be slight variations between batches. Flow Production – this is usually defined as very large numbers of products produced continuously on a production line. It is often referred to as 'Mass Production' or 'Line Production' as the goods are made on production lines.

2 Job production advantages – The product is made to the specific requirements of the customer. High prices can be charged for the skill and expertise involved. Disadvantages – Can take a long time to produce. Production costs are also high because there are no opportunities for economies of scale to be made.

Page 105 Quick Fire Questions

1 'Quality' usually means a product which has been made using high quality raw materials and highly trained staff.

2 Quality control – This involves checking products after they have been produced to make sure they meet the standards expected. Quality circles – This involves bringing groups of employees together with the management, in order to discuss issues of quality. Employees are usually trained to identify, analyse and solve some of the problems in their work.

3   Everyone in the organisation is trained in quality, and they know how to deliver products and services to customers' requirements.

4   Benchmarking is an approach to quality which involves the business applying a set of standards or benchmarks. The business has to make sure that it achieves these benchmarks in order to stay competitive.

5   Very important and accurate feedback can be received about the customer experience, as employees do not know who the mystery shopper is.

Page 105 Sample Examination Question

1   Quality management systems are as follows. Quality control – This involves checking products after they have been produced to make sure they meet the standards expected. Quality assurance – This involves a planned and systematic approach to checking products at more regular intervals during the production process, and trying to avoid problems happening in the first place. Total Quality management – This involves every employee in the organisation ensuring that quality is built in at each and every stage of the production process. Quality standards and symbols – In the UK, there are recognised systems of quality standards (e.g. The BSI (British Standards Institution) which places a Kitemark on products which meet the standard). Benchmarking – Benchmarking is an approach to quality which involves the business applying a set of standards or benchmarks.

Page 107 Quick Fire Questions

1   Fair trade involves giving producers a fair price for their products.

2   Bananas, coffee, chocolate, flowers, cotton, etc.

3   Disadvantages of Fairtrade – Prices are higher, both for the manufacturer who buy fairtrade raw materials and the consumer who buys the final product. Many of the products have to be transported a long way across the world leading to issues of environmental pollution. Benefits of Fairtrade – Customers are happy to buy Fairtrade products so there will be increased customer loyalty. Most businesses who are licensed for Fairtrade enjoy a good reputation and public image, therefore employees are easier to recruit.

4   Ethical behaviour ensures that products are produced in the right way, e.g. not using child labour, paying good wages, following Health and Safety laws and the Equality Act 2010.

5   One benefit of using ethical operations is that customers will have confidence in the business, and therefore sales and profits will increase.

Page 109 Quick Fire Questions

1   Businesses must avoid pollution, dumping of waste and using up limited resources.

2   Recycling helps the environment by allowing waste materials to be reused, also by saving energy and reducing greenhouse gases.

3   Reducing packaging reduces waste and saves on energy. This helps businesses reduce costs, and helps save the environment by using less of the limited resources.

Page 111 Quick Fire Questions

1   Computer Aided Design.

2   Speed, accuracy and continuity and a reduction in the number of employees required therefore saving costs.

3   The EPOS system scans the barcodes on the products, which looks up the price of the item and deducts the item from the total stock balance.

4   For market research purposes, EPOS can gather information very quickly about the shopping habits of customers. The computer can rank the most popular products sold in a day, week, month, etc. It can also total how much is being spent on each item.

5   EPOS can also be used by customers accessing the business website to see if certain items are in stock. They can he held for customers to uplift from the store, or they can be delivered to their homes.

Page 113 Quick Fire Questions

1   Sending emails to customers; asking for replies to certain questions; feedback forms on websites; sending SMS messages, asking for customers to provide ratings; using survey websites such as Survey Monkey.

2   No guarantee that this survey will be read; or technical issues with hardware.

3   Customers experience rapid delivery times as well as lower prices.

4   It allows customers to interact with businesses in their own homes and therefore increase sales.

5   Electronic viral marketing is when information about a product or a business gets passed around very quickly from one person to the next, with a snowball effect.

Page 113 Sample Examination Question

1   The full range of an organisation's products can be shown on a website, therefore the products are available for consumers to look at. Customers can purchase online from their own home which increases sales. It allows worldwide sales in the global economy. Sales can be made 24/7. Reduces costs due to not requiring expensive premises or large amounts of staff. Customers can leave comments on websites. The company can make use of customer details for market research purposes. There is customer satisfaction, with rapid deliveries to their homes and reduced prices.

© 2014 Leckie & Leckie Ltd
Cover © ink-tank

001/21102014

10 9 8 7 6 5 4 3 2 1

ISBN 9780007554430

Published by
Leckie & Leckie Ltd
An imprint of HarperCollins*Publishers*
Westerhill Road, Bishopbriggs, Glasgow, G64 2QT
T: 0844 576 8126   F: 0844 576 8131
leckieandleckie@harpercollins.co.uk   www.leckieandleckie.co.uk

Publisher: Katherine Wilkinson
Project Managers: Craig Balfour & Sonia Dawkins

Special thanks to
Donna Cole (copy edit); Felicity Kendall (proofread);
Ink Tank (cover design); QBS (layout)

Printed in Italy by Lego, S.P.A.

A CIP Catalogue record for this book is available from the
British Library.

Acknowledgements

P20, BBC - mikecphoto/Shutterstock.com; P29, Gordon Strachan
- Tomasz Bidermann/Shutterstock.com; P46, LinkedIn - Atelier_A/
Shutterstock.com; P58, Industrial action - i4lcocl2/Shutterstock.
com; P73, Sold sign - nanka/Shutterstock.com; P92, Point of sale -
"Easter PoS Display". Licensed under Public domain via Wikimedia
Commons - http://commons.wikimedia.org/wiki/File:Easter_PoS_
Display.JPG#mediaviewer/File:Easter_PoS_Display.JPG; P93, Fergie
- Everett Collection/Shutterstock.com; P96, Qantas - Getty Images;
P99, Halifax - Bloomberg via Getty Images; P106, Fairtrade -
Thinglass/Shutterstock.com

All other images © Shutterstock.com

The Publishers would like to thank the companies and
organisations that have agreed for their logos to be used
throughout this publication.

Sample exam questions Copyright © Scottish Qualifications Authority

Whilst every effort has been made to trace the copyright holders,
in cases where this has been unsuccessful, or if any have
inadvertently been overlooked, the Publishers would gladly
receive any information enabling them to rectify any
error or omission at the first opportunity.